WALT DISNEY

Biography

The life of a pioneer in the field of animation

David M Chapin

TABLE OF CONTENTS

PART I: STORIES [OF] MY FATHERS – 1801–1890

Chapter One: Heritage

The greatest characters in history frequently break the mould in their families, either by overcoming adversity to become extraordinary or by using the resources they were given to leave their own particular stamp on the world. These people are usually few and few between, with one person rising to prominence in a familial line.

Walt Disney's ancestors, on the other hand, are an outlier: historians have tracked his ancestors back 1,000 years, and they contain aristocracy and farmers, soldiers and pacifists, criminals and the respectable. His and his family's biography is amazing, spanning millennia across both hemispheres. While the family's social class, career choice, and reason for importance have all changed dramatically over the years, the characteristics that defined the Disneys have always remained the same: hard work, a desire for self-improvement, a dream of progress, a strong loyalty to their country, and a willingness to move to pursue new opportunities when one's luck had run out.

The Disney family can be traced back to Isigny-sur-Mer in the Duchy of Normandy in northwest France, to 1066. The Chateau de Monfreville was owned by a local named Hughes, who had inherited it from a local bishop. Hughes and his family were surrounded by flora and animals at their chateau, seeing dozens of bird species migrate, including storks, swallows, owls, and cuckoos. Badgers and foxes passed by at regular intervals, and there was plenty of wildlife for hunting. Cows owned by local farmers were used for dairy products nearby, while agricultural items grown in enclosures as well as the commons, such as apples, supplied a regular supply of food and by-products such as ciders and vinegars.

When Edward, King of England, died in 1066, his brother-in-law, Harold, Earl of Essex, was crowned his heir. This angered William, Duke of Normandy, who believed he had been given Edward's promise that he would be the next King of England. William chose to invade England to exercise his dominance in order to secure his title to the throne. An order was issued to all landowners, aristocracy, and knights throughout the Duchy of Normandy, commanding them to report for service in fighting for and supporting their duke as the new king of England.

Hughes, as owner of the Chateau de Monfreville, and his son Robert were expected to form part of the invading force that would cross the English Channel to Britain's southern coastlines. When William's armies defeated the opposing claimant's forces at the Battle of Hastings, he awarded his warriors with territory in England; as war survivors, Hughes and Robert were granted property in Lincolnshire, as well as authority as Norman conquerors of English residents. Hughes, Robert, and their family adopted the surname 'd'Isigny' to assert their authority over the natives and to distinguish themselves from the English. This demonstrated that they were from the Norman village and hence more powerful than their neighbours. Over the next few centuries, the family's surname would be reduced and anglicised, ultimately transforming to 'Disney'.

As the Disney family associated themselves with the British royal family, a great devotion to one's country became a recurring theme over the next several centuries. In 1642, King Charles I, who had been striving to govern with absolute authority, was opposed by Parliament, which was attempting to deprive the monarchy of power. The Disneys' devotion to the Crown made it clear whose side to support during the English Civil War. Edward Disney went to war as a Royalist, believing it was his duty to assist the monarch in putting down the rebellious followers of the legislature known as Parliamentarians.

Edward Disney was seized and sent to nearby Warwick Castle when the Royalists were beaten by the Parliamentarians. Because he was a wealthy man, Edward was imprisoned in Guy's Tower, where aristocrats were housed while they awaited execution. The young man had a lot of free time during his six-month confinement, and he came to the conclusion that, while he was facing death as an enemy of the state, he was on the right side. He decided it was time to make his mark on the world as a Royalist martyr, carving his name, 'Edward Disney,' and the year, '1643,' inside an arrow slit set into the room's wall.

However, Edward was not executed: in order to raise funds to finance their fight against Charles and his followers, the Parliamentarians began ransoming prisoners back to their families. Edward Disney was one of the ransomed captives who returned home to his family.

Following Charles I's death and Oliver Cromwell's seizure of power, the Disneys realised they were on the wrong side of the struggle. After selling their properties in England in the 1660s, the family relocated to County Louth, Ireland, north of Dublin, and then a few decades later to County Kilkenny. It was here that the Disney family proclaimed its noble ancestry once more, renting more than 30 acres of land for the expanding family. As a result of their affluence, they frequently wielded political authority, even serving as mayors or collecting tolls at numerous ports throughout Ireland.

Kepple and Frances Best Disney welcomed their son, Arundel Elias Disney, to their Kilkenny estate in 1801. It was here that young Arundel, who went by the name Elias, acquired an education appropriate for his social standing. His father's money and status enabled him to get an education, which was considered a luxury in the early nineteenth century. Furthermore, the family had no need for anything, relying on a lot of staff to look after them.

Elias grew up and fell in love with a local girl, Maria Swan, who was thirteen years his junior. While his family was not thrilled with his son marrying Maria because she hailed from a lower-status family than the Disneys, they recognized that she was of good birth and thus permitted the union. Elias and Maria married in 1832, and their son, Kepple, was born on November 2 of that year.

Elias and his brother Robert discovered business opportunities in New York City, USA, a few years later. The two young men sold their farms and travelled to Liverpool with their wives and children. Elias Disney and his six companions embarked aboard a huge steamer, The New Jersey, in mid-September 1834, and arrived in New York City on October 3, 1834.

While Robert and his family chose to stay in New York to pursue business prospects, Elias and Maria travelled on to Canada. They'd heard that the Canada Company was selling parcels of property in Ontario, boasting that the cheap land was exceptionally productive and ready for agriculture. In their advertisements, the corporation also stated that the area surrounding Goderich Township had full facilities, such as roads, companies to serve the inflow of settlers, and infrastructure. Elias bought a plot of property in Goderich, near Holmesville, along the Maitland River, to start a farm. He obtained it through a Crown Grant issued by the Canada Company, which means that his family purchased the land directly from the government rather than from a prior owner. He had two distinct parcels totaling 149 acres by 1842, where he farmed wheat. When he arrived, he was disappointed to discover that he had been misled: there were few to no facilities in the region. Goderich Township had few structures and no church, and the land he had purchased had not been cleared as promised. As a result, because Elias Disney's land was previously undeveloped, he recognized the need for an alternative strategy to feed his family. He began work on constructing a gristmill and a sawmill along the Maitland River, using the river's currents to power the mills and opening them to the public.

Life on the frontier was extremely different from the grandeur and privilege that Elias Disney had grown accustomed to in Ireland. However, he and Maria rapidly learned to adapt to the bountiful natural resources to care for the family. Wild fruit like grapes and plums flourished abundantly, while Elias and young Kepple relied on the Maitland for fishing and the forest for wild wildlife. However, life on the Canadian border was not without dangers: it was not uncommon for men in the area to fend off packs of wolves that presented a threat to their families or livestock.

Kepple married a local girl, Mary Richardson, whose family had also emigrated from Ireland, when he reached marriageable age. Soon after their marriage in 1858, the newlyweds relocated to Bluevale, a little community some 50 kilometres from their parents' home in Holmesville. Within a year, Mary became pregnant with her first child, Elias Disney, who was born on February 6, 1859. Kepple developed a farm near Bluevale, complemented by other money-making endeavours, with the assumption that their family would continue to grow. When drilling for oil proved unsuccessful, Kepple was relieved to discover that his property held salt instead, and he constructed the area's first salt mine.

Kepple and Mary had seven more children during the next eighteen years. As the oldest son, Elias recognized the value of being a family leader, utilising the education he obtained at the local public school as well as the moral and religious training provided at the Wesleyan Methodist Church and Sunday School. This schooling, together with Kepple and Mary's Christian upbringing, equipped Elias and his brothers with moral and physical fortitude, teaching them the qualities of hard work, ethical purity, honesty, and frugality.

While attending the Wesleyan Methodist Church and the local public school, young Elias pursued a passion that he knew would be frowned upon by his conservative family. When he requested Kepple and Mary for permission to learn to play the violin, they laughed at him, telling him that it was an instrument played by the devil himself and that no son of theirs would pursue such an immoral hobby. In an act of defiance, the young guy snuck away into the woods to practise the fiddle away from the sight and earshot of authority. This, however, did not endure long. Grandma Maria heard the dance sounds ringing through the trees one afternoon. She discovered her eldest grandchild on a log playing the sinful instrument after following the sound of the terrible music. She went up, seized it from the boy's grasp, and brought it down over his head before he could object, leaving the instrument a heap of smashed pieces and shattered wood.

Kepple's financial success began to wane in 1877, prompting him to seek other chances. Mary was expecting once more, which meant there would be another mouth to feed shortly. The news had spread that there was still time to strike it rich in the goldfields of California and the silver fields of the American West. Kepple, Elias, and their second son Robert crossed the Canadian border into the American Midwest, aiming toward the Pacific, where wealth beckoned.

A Union Pacific Railroad salesman contacted Kepple and his sons on a train headed west from Missouri, offering them a land grant. Kepple began the process of placing his boys on a parcel of a few

9

hundred acres of land along Big Creek in the new railroad town of Ellis, Kansas, by sending for Mary and the rest of the children.

Kepple Disney and his family were not the first ones to begin settling west of the Mississippi. In the midst of the American Civil War in 1862, President Abraham Lincoln signed the Homestead Act, with the goal of "elevating the condition of men, lifting artificial burdens from all shoulders, and giving everyone an unfettered start and a fair chance in the race of life." This land was made available to American citizens at a low cost: 160-acre portions were offered to pioneers for a simple $18 application fee. To keep the land, homesteaders had to live on it for five years, farm it, and make improvements such as digging a well or building a road. While the Homestead Act was a relative success for Americans (over 270 million acres were settled over the next 124 years), it drove thousands of Native Americans off the land they had inhabited for generations, forcing them to relocate to less desirable plots or even to reservations.

Unfortunately, Kepple and Mary Disney were not citizens of the United States. As a result, they were unable to take advantage of the Homestead Act's low-cost land offer fifteen years after Lincoln signed it. The great railroad lines that were moving west across the continent, on the other hand, presented a solution: their own land concessions.

Because of the huge number of railroad firms, railroad corporations had no way of producing an instant profit, and it was also difficult to attract investors. Because it was their development that was essentially driving the rise of heavy industry in the United States in the second half of the nineteenth century, railroad businesses sought aid from the federal government.

While the government did not provide them with free financial appropriations, it did supply them with land grants totaling 20 square miles for each mile of track built. These land concessions might be divided as the companies saw fit and then sold to individuals or households to help fund the construction of the railways. In the 1870s and 1880s, railroads saw a particularly lucrative opportunity as large numbers of people, both American and immigrant, including Kepple and Mary Disney, began to migrate west in search of cheap land and new prospects. Railroad corporations in the American West were granted nearly 130 million acres in 1871, accounting for 7% of the total amount of land controlled by the United States at the time.

Kepple and his family had a difficult time in Ellis, Kansas. As a halt on the Union Pacific Railroad's Kansas Pacific line, the town quickly became a loading post for cattle being driven from pasture land in Texas and New Mexico and delivered east to Chicago. As a result, crime and alcoholism became common among visitors to the town. Ellis residents frequently engaged in debauchery and other vices given to visiting cattle drives, such as the town's thriving prostitute industry. Except for the morally honest Elias, Kepple and his sons abandoned their conservative character in Canada and succumbed to Ellis's temptations, frequenting both saloons and prostitutes.

Native American raids were also common in the town. Angry at being forced off the ground they had occupied for generations, Native American tribes believed that the only way to force white Americans to leave their country was to attack: diplomacy had failed over the past five decades.

Elias took refuge from the railroad town's temptations in the local church, which did far more than just provide sermons on Sunday mornings. Churches in American frontier towns frequently served as the region's social core, where inhabitants would gather to swap news and gossip, and social activities such as picnics and camp meetings were held. The centrally positioned church in Ellis provided Elias with an opportunity to meet with others who were struggling to resist the temptations of the brothel and saloon. It also reinforced the character values established in him by his childhood, making him even more dedicated to honest, hard labour, and a thoroughly moral lifestyle.

After arriving in Ellis, the Disneys were not well off. They had to buy the equipment, animals, seeds, and other things needed to start their farm after paying the Kansas Pacific for their plot of property; establishing the farm was of the utmost importance, as it was farming that would assist the family produce money so they could exist. With eleven mouths to feed (Mary had given birth to her ninth child in March 1878, just before Kepple sent for her to join him in Kansas), there wasn't much money left after the grocery payment.

Kansas' topography was quite flat, and the grassland environment was covered in shortgrass. As a result, hardwoods and lumber are more expensive to obtain, making normal home construction challenging. Following in the footsteps of their German neighbours who had arrived in Ellis, the Disney family began to build a house out of prairie sod. Kepple and his sons scooped down the hill sloping down to Big Creek's banks, stacking rectangular clumps of sod as the structure's walls. The prairie grass in these clumps held the dirt together, and the dry summer heat eventually baked the sod into brick. The trusses for the roof were hewn from a few scattered cottonwood trees that grew along the creek; these, after being covered with lighter clumps of earth, kept the occasional rain from wetting the packed earth floor of the dwelling. This prairie building style not only allowed for the construction of a home in an area devoid of typical building materials, but it was also beneficial in protecting against the harsh conditions of the region's climate: the partially underground nature of the structure helped to keep the house cool in the blistering summer heat, while the earth bricks allowed for insulation against the freezing winter temperatures. This rudimentary cabin, however, was only temporary: once Kepple and Mary had achieved some success on the farm and had saved enough money, they quickly invested in building a house out of stone obtained from a nearby quarry.

Elias, dissatisfied with his father's employment, left the tiny wheat and cattle farm Kepple had developed and began looking for work elsewhere. It was time to break free from his past and seize the prospects that America provided for him and any future Disneys ready to dream of a better life in the world.

Chapter Two: Elias and Flora

As Elias Disney entered his second decade, he left his mother, father, siblings, and sisters to join the great march west by partnering with the booming railroad industry. He quickly found work at a machine shop for the Kansas Pacific Railroad, putting to use the skills he had learned while working at Kepple's gristmill and sawmill in Ontario, as well as repairing broken machinery and farming implements on the farm in Ellis. The Kansas Pacific Railroad was a branch of the Union Pacific Railroad, which was founded in 1838. America began its push west across the American prairies in the early nineteenth century, fueled by the doctrine of Manifest Destiny, which declared that it was God's plan for the American people to conquer the North American continent from the Atlantic to the Pacific. Suggestions were made to build a transcontinental railroad across North America connecting the two coasts in order to facilitate the easy transfer of people and materials west. Congress laughed at the concept, claiming that building such a railroad would be as absurd as building one from Earth to the moon.

Travelling through the wilderness was difficult prior to the development of the major railways, and was generally done by wagon and draught horse. Travelling west frequently took several days, weeks, or even months because the ungainly creatures struggled to cross the hills, mountains, woods, and muddy pathways. Following the migration of immigrants to California in the 1840s and 1850s in search of gold and other precious metals, proponents for a rail line encouraged prospectors to petition Congress for a train that would connect them to the east, making travel back and forth easier. A number of debates in the legislature over the idea of a transcontinental railroad stalled following sectionally motivated arguments over whether the train's eastern end would be in the American north or south.

Finally, in 1853, the United States Congress passed legislation authorising the start of geological surveys for a transcontinental railroad running from St. Louis, Missouri to California. To complete the task of building the railroad, two railroad corporations emerged: the Central Pacific Railroad, which began construction east from Sacramento, California in January 1863, and the Union Pacific Railroad, which began construction west from Omaha, Nebraska the following December. While the two railroad companies originally planned to build separate railroads across America, it was quickly agreed that the two train lines would meet and connect to form a single transcontinental route.

The Central Pacific and Union Pacific Railroads met at Promontory Summit in Utah on May 10, 1869. A ceremony marked America's first transcontinental railroad's historic achievement: as a locomotive from each railroad was drawn towards the junction of the two lines, a ceremonial golden spike was driven to tie the rails together, indicating the project's completion. The word spread quickly across the country as Americans hailed the historic milestone. Five days later, regular service over the Transcontinental Railroad commenced.

This successful endeavour motivated other railroad firms to grow and strive for success similar to that of the Central Pacific and Union Pacific Railroads. It was also quickly realised that other parts of the country needed to be connected to the transcontinental line, which only went from Sacramento to Omaha. As a result, additional railroads such as the Atchison, Topeka & Santa Fe, the Denver & Rio Grande, and the Missouri, Kansas & Texas Railroads began to connect to the long line.

The Union Pacific Eastern Division, which began construction in 1855, became a southern railroad line running parallel to the Transcontinental Railroad in 1863. However, the Eastern Division changed its name to the Kansas Pacific Railroad five years later, establishing a major rail line from Kansas City, Kansas in the east to Denver, Colorado in the west. Kepple Disney bought his farm in Ellis from this clan.

When young Elias Disney heard the thrilling stories of those who were constructing the train line across the American frontier, he quickly left the Kansas Pacific machine shop. Instead, he elected to work on the new line's construction from Ellis to its end in Denver, where it curved north to link with the Union Pacific. Along the way, Elias became aware of the corruption that big business wielded over the poor and marginalised, especially immigrants. While gaining American citizenship after Kepple and Mary were naturalised the year before, he witnessed the horrible treatment and working circumstances endured by many of the railroad workers. Building a new railroad through the plains and mountains could be highly dangerous, therefore company officials frequently relied on immigrants for labour, including Irish and Germans on the eastern lines and Chinese on the western lines.

Many of the labourers found themselves out of work after the line was completed in Denver. Elias, unwilling to return to Kepple's farm in Ellis, decided to buy another fiddle and use his talent to entertain Denver residents by performing outside saloons. Unfortunately, when this did not result in success, he opted to return home to Kansas, feeling quite discouraged about his future.

Fortunately, fate was on Elias' side. While he returned to work on Kepple's farm, his younger sister Annie began teaching at the Beaver Bank School in Ellis in 1884, under the headmaster, Charles Call. Call had left his childhood home in the mid-1800s to accompany the gold rush to California. When his quest yielded no results, he returned east, settling in Ellis in 1879 and opened Beaver Bank School for the developing town's students.

Elias occasionally substituted for his sister, which allowed him to get to know Call and the students at the school. He quickly became acquainted with Call's daughter Flora, a bright 16-year-old who excelled academically, including a perfect score on her end-of-year exams in her advanced class in 1881. Elias began spending more time with Charles Call and his family during the next few years, and he began to pursue a connection with Flora.

Flora graduated as Beaver Bank's valedictorian from high school. A few years later, at the school's commencement (similar to graduation), she delivered a speech that was timely for a young girl growing up in an American frontier town: "Neglect not the Gift that is in Thee." The young woman acknowledged that everyone was endowed with some sort of gift and that it was their responsibility to nurture that gift in order to fulfil their destiny.

Charles Call and his wife Henrietta sold their land in Ellis and relocated to Akron, Florida, after their daughter graduated. Kepple, who had met the Calls through his children's friendship with the family, decided to accompany them to examine potential in the area. Elias, who was head over heels in love with Flora, decided to accompany his father. Kepple's eldest son decided to stay behind owing to his budding infatuation with Flora Call when he saw

Kansas presented greater possibilities for his family. Elias began aggressively courting Flora after purchasing 80 acres of farmland in nearby Kismet, and the two married on January 1, 1888, in the Call family house in Akron.

The newlyweds purchased an extra 150 acres and many head of cattle from Elias' farms in Kismet. Unfortunately, a sickness ran across the herd, and when many of the cows perished, Elias realised that cattle raising was not for him. The couple moved to Daytona Beach, where they ran the Halifax Hotel during the 1888 tourist season, after the new husband sold his farm. When autumn arrived and the tourists went, the hotel owner no longer needed his manager and forced Elias and Flora to vacate their room. This was especially tough for the couple because Flora was expecting her first child in December.

Elias quickly realised he needed to find a job in order to support his increasing family. He got a part-time job as a postal carrier for the town of Kissimmee and also bought about 160 acres of land to try to create an orange plantation. This, however, did not offer a significant income.

Later that autumn, Elias Disney enlisted in the Florida militia: a surge of patriotism had swept the country in recent years, as talk of conflict with Spain began to spread. While Spain had owned the Caribbean island of Cuba since the fifteenth century, Cubans began to want independence in the late 1870s. José Mart, a Cuban exile, began rallying Cubans in west and south Florida to support his cause. While the United States despised the Spanish treatment of Cubans, the administration regarded a potential Cuban revolution as an opportunity to conquer the island as part of the emerging American empire in the Western hemisphere. To ensure Cuban 'success,' clearing the way for American annexation, the notion of America as the rescuer of the Spanish Empire spread throughout the country. This was a result of articles published by American newspaper magnates Joseph Pulitzer and William Randolph Hearst during their violent competition to sell papers, including practices such as sensationalising news events in order to increase subscriptions, which became known as 'yellow journalism'. These ideals persuaded young and old alike to enlist in the United States military forces and local state militias in preparation for war, which finally broke out in 1898.

After several weeks of training at the militia base, Elias realised that military life wasn't for him: the severe discipline conflicted with his personality, and his fellow soldiers' behaviour and language didn't mesh with his conservative Methodist ideals. Flora's written letter also revealed that the new mother was struggling to keep the orange grove running while caring for a newborn: Flora had given birth to a boy, Herbert Arthur, on December 8. The young father made the decision to leave the camp and return to Kissimmee.

A few days later, some U.S. Army officers appeared at their front door, ready to apprehend the young deserter. However, Elias refused to accompany the authorities.

"I didn't desert," he stated emphatically. "I volunteered for this outfit, which means I can just as easily un-volunteer." This drew the attention of the United States. Army cops are caught off surprise. "We'll need your uniform then, sir," they said. "You do not have my uniform. "I paid for it with my own money, so it's mine," Elias said. Not anticipating such opposition, and realising the young man was completely correct, the police officers departed the Disney property, allowing the deserter to go free. A record frost hit across central Florida a few weeks later, dusting the orange trees on the Disney property. Elias had hoped that some of the oranges would be saved, so he started out right once to reclaim some of his trees. He became ill in the midst of his hard effort and was diagnosed with malaria. Fed up with his dismal luck in Florida, the new father began to hunt for work abroad.

In 1890, prominent political and cultural elites in the United States proposed commemorating the 400th anniversary of Columbus' discovery of America. Inspired by the Exposition Universelle de Paris the previous year, it was decided that the United States needed its own version of an exposition to commemorate the historic occasion. While most people agreed that Washington, D.C. Other significant cities in America realised that hosting the fair would bring respect and improve their prominence both in the country and beyond the world. St. Louis, Missouri, and New York City both bid to host the fair. Cultural leaders in Chicago wished that the fair be held in their city because they considered it best embodied the American spirit following the Great Chicago Fire of 1871. Following a vote in the American Congress on February 24, 1890, it was decided that Chicago would be the site of the World's Columbian Exposition of 1893.

The fairgrounds were to be built at Jackson Park, southeast of downtown Chicago and along the shores of Lake Michigan. Designed by Frederick Law Olmstead, best known for his work on New York's Central Park, Jackson Park was the city's attempt to bring beauty to the urban region. Unfortunately, the park's location near Lake Michigan exacerbated the problem of sand hills blown in from the lake, as well as massive spinning cesspools caused by increasing tides. The decision to bring Olmstead back to Chicago to design the fairground was an attempt to address Jackson Park's issues while also bringing in a worldwide famous landscape architect to attract people to the fair.

Burnham & Root, a well-known architectural firm, was hired to design the fair's buildings. The carnival was classical in nature, with soaring columns, high domes, and wide arcades, while fountains, statuary, and small lakes added grace to the industrial exposition. Chicago, dubbed 'The White City' due to the pure and classical colour of the buildings, served as a place where sophisticated and advanced culture could be displayed, demonstrating the ability of 1890s America to overcome the temptations and vice of the period.

To keep himself occupied while recovering from malaria, Elias would read the newspaper. He frequently spotted posters for work in the Carpenters and Building Association's temporary structures in Jackson Park for the fair. This prospect piqued the young man's interest: Chicago would be a fresh start. He was sick of rural life and the lack of consistent work; he saw how difficult it was for his father to start the farm in Ellis, remembered being laid off upon arriving in Denver while working on the Kansas Pacific, and was extremely frustrated and slightly depressed about the fate of his orange grove in Kissimmee. A huge northern metropolis provided new opportunities:

solid work, a higher standard of living, good schools for Herbert, and the possibility of a better life with access to existing infrastructure and new technologies. His younger brother Robert had already settled in Chicago and was looking for land on the city's south side to develop a hotel near Jackson Park. This meant that establishing himself would be a little easier because he could draw on Robert's experience to help him acclimate.

Besides, he reasoned, Chicago wouldn't be an altogether different experience. Chicago was far enough east to have a history and to have witnessed American industrial development. As the centre of the animal slaughter and meatpacking business in the United States, it was served by hundreds of rail lines. However, Chicago was far enough west that it was newer than locations like New York, Philadelphia, and Washington, D.C., so there were many options for jobs and building a name for oneself. According to his understanding, there were still open stretches of prairie land just north and west of the city, implying the prospect of property ownership as well as the use of some of the skills he had learned working on his father's land back west. Not only that, but as a booming city, it looked to draw many respectable immigrants, such as the German community he had grown to know in Kansas.

The couple's decision was influenced by an unanticipated family tragedy. Flora's father, Charles Call, was seriously injured in an accident while clearing his Florida acreage of pine trees in 1890, and died a few weeks later. His death made Elias and Flora's decision to leave Florida that much simpler. So, in late spring 1890, they packed their belongings and relocated to Chicago to find work in the fairgrounds of the World's Columbian Exposition, which was set to open in three years. Elias was convinced that he would finally get secure work, but he didn't realise that his possibilities were slim: contrary to what The Rights of Labor advertised, there was no plethora of jobs. According to later figures, for every job opening for construction at the fairgrounds, applicants would have to compete with at least ten other men. These were the circumstances that the Disneys, along with almost 25,000 other families, found themselves in.

PART II: I'LL NAME MINE AFTER YOU – CHICAGO, ILLINOIS, 1890–1906

Chapter Three: The White City

Elias, Flora, and Herbert were not the only ones who relocated to Chicago. The three Disneys were accompanied by their unborn second kid on their long journey north from Florida to Chicago. Flora was just a few months pregnant when her family landed in Illinois.

Elias didn't spend any time choosing a new home for their growing family. Because he recognized the transient nature of the labour available at the World's Columbian Exposition, he persuaded Flora that they should rent rather than buy a house. Their second son, Raymond Arnold, was born on December 30, 1890, at 3515 Vernon Avenue, south of downtown Chicago. The house's location was determined as much by the need for extra room as it was by Elias's new job working at the world's fair: it was roughly twenty blocks, or about two miles, from the fairgrounds, on the southern side of Washington Park. As a result, he found it rather easy to come to work every day, either by walking or taking the trams that ran down the Midway Plaisance, a boulevard bordered by a greenway that connected Washington Park to Jackson Park, the site of the exposition. As the fair's construction progressed, Elias found himself walking past exhibits such as recreations of authentic villages from around the world, a Californian Ostrich Farm restaurant, a tethered balloon that carried passengers 60 metres into the air, and venues for various performances such as animal shows and belly dancers. The World Columbian Exposition's response to Gustave Eiffel's Tower at the Exposition Universelle de Paris in 1889, however, was most remarkable to those passing through the Midway Plaisance: an 80-metre wheel bearing the name of its designer, George Washington Gale Ferris.

The construction of the World's Columbian Exposition was not always easy. Elias appeared to be earning more money than he was likely getting in Florida. His daily wage was roughly $1 (equivalent to about $28 in today's money). However, this was significantly lower than the national average for carpenters. In actuality, carpenters in the United States were paid an average of $2.52 per day for their labour. Unfortunately for Elias and his colleagues preparing the fairgrounds for the Exposition's 1893 opening, the fair's construction management required a big supply of carpenters and other labourers, allowing them to pay their workers poor rates. Any employee who voiced displeasure with the required long hours or poor compensation could be promptly fired in favour of another candidate who would be happy with the same long hours and low pay. The problems and disappointments caused by poor working conditions and inadequate pay were exacerbated by the difficulties of winter. Temperatures averaged -23°C in early 1892, while the winter of 1893 was even worse. Some formed labour unions to advocate for better treatment.

Several industrial confrontations erupted in the Chicago area during the early 1890s, many of which were directly related to the economic downturn. When the company's owner, George Pullman, reduced the wages of his workers, a walkout broke out at the Pullman factory in Gary, Indiana. This was extremely tough for his employees because they not only worked for Pullman, but also rented their homes and purchased their food from him: Pullman owned the entire town where his factory was located. As a result, while salaries fell, rent and food prices remained stable, putting a pressure on the working poor who worked in Pullman's factories. When the workers threatened to organise, the billionaire banned labour unions and laid off 75% of his workforce, replacing them with labourers willing to work for considerably lower wages.

The financial impact on Gary's workers was severe, and many suffered from homelessness, a shortage of food, or an insufficient supply of fuel to heat their houses. Eugene V. Debs, a labour organiser, arrived in Gary at this period, ready to fight for workers' rights. Debs helped to organise the workers into an official union, encouraging them to strike and lobbying other members of the American Railway Union across the country to boycott the Pullman railroad cars. As a result of the boycott, rumours began to circulate that the American train system would stop transporting products and people, as well as slowing the delivery of mail across the country.

The protests quickly turned violent after Debs defied a federal injunction, leading the government to send troops to occupy Chicago, allowing trains to pass through unmolested.

While the strikers lost the battle with George Pullman, their efforts were noticed by others in the city and across the country. Laws began to change, prohibiting youngsters from working and instead mandating them to attend obligatory school until they reached the age of 14. Exposition writers, such as Lincoln Steffens, began touring major cities. Steffens criticised Chicago in his book, The Shame of the Cities, for being the most violent and filthiest city in the country. As the middle and working classes grew weary of the American laissez-faire capitalist system, leaders like Debs gained followers, advocating for socialist-style governments and putting public ownership of railroads and utilities critical to American livelihoods.

Debs himself visited Chicago during the time he fought with the strikers at the Pullman factory, recognizing his responsibilities to fight for the large city's industrial workers, many of whom were immigrants and thus easy to exploit through low salaries. He supported Chicago's industrial workers through his organisation, the Industrial Workers of the World, which was frequently accused of being socialist by its opponents and industry leadership. He was joined in his quest for improved working conditions by other labour organisations, such as the American Federation of Labor, a craft union, and the Knights of Labor, which embraced all workers, skilled and unskilled alike. While the American Federation of Labor was a newer organisation when compared to the Knights of Labor around the turn of the century, it swiftly eclipsed the latter in terms of membership due to its appeal to urban middle-class Americans, particularly native-born white Americans. In the early 1890s, Elias Disney worked in this political, social, and industrial climate, which influenced his opinions toward labour and large business for decades to come.

Elias realised that his position as a carpenter at the fair would only be temporary when he accepted it. As a result, he began creating furniture for local markets using the skills he learned on the

Transcontinental Railroad and polished in Chicago.

Elias purchased a 7.62m by 38.1m property in Northwest Town, now known as Kelvyn Grove, a suburb outside Chicago, in 1891, with money he and Flora had saved from his labour at the World's Columbian Exposition and sales of his handmade furniture. The pair agreed to build the house together: Flora would design it and Elias would build it. When Elias and Flora bought the land, the neighbourhood was still relatively new; originally settled around 1885, the area became a popular place to live for German, Scottish, and Swedish immigrants due to a nearby railroad station, where they could be whisked away to the city's numerous manufacturing centres. The region was annexed by the city of Chicago in 1889, and the neighbourhood was given a new official name: Hermosa.

The global economy experienced a dip as the opening of the World's Columbian Exposition approached. As early as January 20, 1891, major banks in Kansas City, Missouri, failed, causing concern among millions of Americans. At the World's Columbian Exposition, union officials and labourers utilised this as an opportunity to negotiate higher salaries and an eight-hour workweek. Instead of negotiating, the fair construction leadership, led by Daniel Hudson Burnham, hired Italian immigrants to begin building on a ditch at Jackson Park. In response, more than 2,000 enraged workers assaulted the worksite armed with sharpened sticks on February 12, 1891. Protesters kidnapped and battered two Italian workers until police officers arrived to break up the fighting.

The Disney family became personally involved in labour-related violence at the fairgrounds. Elias saw a small group of recently laid off workers beating up a still-employed carpenter on his way to work one morning as he approached his worksite; the angry men were enraged that their victim had kept his job despite accepting his employer's low pay, while they had been fired because of their union cooperation. While blows and kicks rained down from above, the man cowered on the ground, unsuccessfully shielding his head and neck. As the well-aimed kicks broke open the screaming man's skin, blood spilled and pooled nearby. While Elias felt awful for his coworker, he opted to keep going quietly; with his increasing family, he needed revenue from work, no matter how little his boss paid him. Unfortunately, he was discovered, and the group abandoned their first victim to pursue their second. Elias didn't look back or go faster because he didn't want to show how afraid he was. As his legs crumpled beneath him and he fell to the ground, a dark flash flashed across his field of view. Elias' senses wandered as he lay dazed on the dusty road, his eyes registering a shovel being dropped alongside him. The dark stain of his blood was smeared on the spade, and his ringing ears picked up the sound of shouts and cursing from his attackers. Curling up to shield his critical parts, Elias waited for what seemed like an eternity for the onslaught to cease as other men on their way to work raced to his aid and his assailants fled. While Elias wanted to present a tough image by continuing to work, his foreman saw the seriousness of the man's injuries and sent him home for the day to rest. It's also possible that Elias's supervisor didn't want the injured man to draw unwelcome attention, which could lead to further unrest or attacks on his workplace.

With increased police presence, strikers backed down from violent protest and instead turned to negotiation with exposition officials, beginning talks on 14 February to demand an eight-hour workday, wages in accordance with the union pay scale, and the expectation that union labourers would be hired ahead of non-unionised or immigrant workers. When the fair's administration agreed to the eight-hour workday demand but stated that they would consider the others, union officials threatened to organise unions worldwide to oppose the Exposition.

Unfortunately, the American economy did not favour labourers. The Chicago work market has continued to deteriorate, leaving over 25,000 unemployed on the streets. Burnham implemented stronger agreements with subcontractors erecting structures at the Jackson Park fairgrounds, establishing firm deadlines with hefty financial penalties for each day a deadline was not reached. These increased expectations reinforced the fair's construction manager's attitude: for over a year, a sign in his office had ordered workers to 'Rush' because the sluggish rate of construction would prevent the Exposition from opening on time.

In the same year, 1891, Elias learned that his father, Kepple Disney, died in Kansas at the age of 59, leaving the family farm in Ellis to his wife Mary. Elias's sadness is likely to have added to the stress he was experiencing at work.

Throughout 1892, the economy sank further as more banks and businesses collapsed and went out of business. Fair officials, who were already over budget, recognized the need to cut costs and proceeded to slash worker wages and lay off personnel. Burnham was accused of discriminating against union workers by Samuel Gompers, the founder and president of the American Federation of Labor. In an effort to save face during a period of union strife, the chief of construction delegated the investigation to a subordinate, superintendent of construction Dion Geraldine. At the same time, in order to demonstrate to Gompers that he did not discriminate against unions, Burnham directed the various construction department leaders to terminate anyone who was inefficient or performing low quality work. These were mostly non-unionized labourers, as the American Federation of Labor usually safeguarded skilled workers who did good work. Burnham also directed that all carpentry for the fair and its buildings be performed by employees of contracting firms selected directly by exhibition executives. As a result, any carpenters who were not employed by these enterprises were immediately laid off, satiating some of Gompers' and other union leaders' demands.

Labour unrest persisted until the spring of 1893, when union workers walked off the job, refusing to finish the fair until they obtained a minimum salary. Burnham consented to the minimum wage requirement, as well as overtime compensation for any extra hours worked, after threats and counter-threats.

Unfortunately for everyone involved, on 3 May 1893, a Wall Street panic prompted stock prices to drop and banks and businesses to lock their doors. The Pennsylvania and Reading Railroad declared bankruptcy, and the National Cordage Company followed suit. More than 16,000 enterprises and 500 banks had fallen by the end of 1893, leaving nearly 20% of America's employable population unemployed. Fear of financial insecurity drove hundreds of thousands of Americans to become more frugal with their money, resulting in poor attendance rates during the World's Columbian Exposition's early days. Fortunately for the construction workers preparing for the fair, their job was completed until the conclusion of the fair's season in October, so many unionised carpenters escaped probable layoffs.

Elias' employment as a carpenter for the World's Columbian Exposition was lost during the 1893 recession. The layoff was unsurprising; winter was generally a slow time for carpenters and construction workers due to frigid northern temperatures, resulting in increased competition for positions. However, the constant job in Jackson Park at better salaries than he was used to was a boon to Elias and Flora. In fact, when Flora announced she was expecting their third child, Elias was so excited about the financial security that working at the fair gave that he petitioned Flora to name the child Columbus. Flora stated that she would think about it.

The World's Columbian Exposition opened on May 1, 1893. The pomp and ceremony surrounding the first day of the fair was bittersweet for Elias: his layoff from the fairgrounds construction team was sad, but the opportunity to commemorate all his hard work was rewarding. While the Disneys were not among the crowds gathered at Jackson Park on that first day, the good fortune of being in the right place at the right time allowed them to participate in a way that many of the fairgoers could not.

Twenty-three black carriages queued up in front of the Lexington Hotel on Michigan Avenue in Chicago early on May 1. The cars carried a number of local, national, and international officials, including the mayor of Chicago, President Grover Cleveland, and the Duke of Veragua, a descendant of Christopher Columbus, and his wife, the Infanta Eulalia of Spain. More than 200,000 Chicagoans on foot or in various vehicles followed the carriages, followed by more than 1,500 members of the Columbian Guard (members of the security organisation charged for maintaining calm at the fair). This mass of parading humanity turned east, past the home of Elias and Flora Disney, and made their way down the Avenue of Nations in the Midway Plaisance to Jackson Park, where the official opening ceremonies would take place. One can understand Elias Disney's pride, not just as a Chicagoan, but also as someone who had put his heart and soul into building the White City, as he watched the great procession pass by while working on furniture outside his leased home.

However, the Disneys' stay near the fairgrounds and Midway Plaza was only temporary. Flora had been hard at work drawing up drawings for the new home since Elias purchased the site in Hermosa in 1891. It would be a two-story structure in the worker's cottage design popular in Chicago's suburbs. The first floor hallway led to a narrow wooden staircase. A parlour/living room on the right had wide bay windows in the front that let in natural light. The back of the house contained a dining room big enough for a family of five, as well as a kitchen with a water pump and a cook stove. There were three bedrooms upstairs: one large enough for Herb and Ray, one smaller for the new baby, and a beautiful master bedroom with a very large closet. While the house was nothing extravagant, the fact that it was created by the Disneys themselves made it a very memorable residence. Flora finished her blueprints on November 23, 1892, giving Elias the go-ahead to begin construction in earnest. When Flora announced her pregnancy, her husband realised he didn't have as much time as he had hoped to build: the current house in Vernon wouldn't be big enough for the increasing family.

Elias was particularly pleased with the new house's features. While designed in the modest steep-gabled worker's cottage form, the house's timber siding was painted white and embellished with vivid blue trim, a favourite colour choice for the wealthy's American Victorian-style palaces. The house was located at the crossroads of Tripp Avenue and Forty-Second Avenue, the only paved roads in the region. Due to the difficulties of digging up paved roads, especially at the turn of the century, the municipal government of Chicago chose to construct better, longer-lasting water and sewer connections with the paving of roadways. As a result, the Disneys' home at 1249 Tripp Avenue was the first in the neighbourhood to have running water as well as an indoor toilet, which was housed in a small cupboard behind the stairs to the second story. This was unusual: only 43% of homes had inside toilets in the early 1900s.

The house was ultimately built in late spring 1893 for around $800, and Elias was fatigued; he had been working extra hard in the evenings and on weekends as soon as he concluded work at Jackson Park. The layoff from the construction crew had turned out to be a blessing in disguise; while he was no longer employed, the lack of professional employment allowed him to build the house before his third child arrived.

This exodus from Chicago's downtown to the suburbs was a prevalent tendency among the middle and upper classes during this time period. With the advent of thousands of new immigrants to large urban regions in the United States, those rich enough left their mansions and residences on 'the Avenues' along Lake Michigan's coastlines and began extending to newly-developed suburbs north and west of the city. The mansions were turned into multi-family tenement dwellings, while a new sort of community of platted, or planned, suburbs permitted the well-to-do and working classes to separate themselves from what they considered "undesirables." These new neighbourhoods established a small-town atmosphere within walking distance of the city's activities and facilities. It built a community for inhabitants that enriched the culture of the working- and middle-class family by giving shops, better schools and churches, and social life possibilities for the homogeneous residents of the neighbourhoods. When real estate developers for the suburbs explained that the laws of the developments forbade saloons, they drew the city's best and 'the right kind of citizens' that respectable Chicagoans would want for their neighbours.

Flora gave birth to a child on June 24, 1893, just after the Disneys moved into their new house. Elias reminded her of his request that the baby be named Columbus. She objected, instead going by the name Roy. However, the issue of naming the baby's middle name continued. Flora was sitting with her baby in her new home's front parlour one day when she spotted a large timber truck driving along Tripp Avenue outside the bay window, most likely dumping off wood for new home construction. The company's name was boldly painted over the side of the truck: Oliver Lumber Company. The pair agreed that 'Roy Oliver' went well together, putting an end to Elias' wish to pay homage to the Exposition.

Things were not as easy for the couple with their third kid as they had been with the prior two. Roy was always fussy and frequently ill, and it was quickly determined that he couldn't digest milk. When affluent Aunt Margaret, Elias's brother Robert's wife, found out, she wrote to a doctor in Boston who had treated her when she was younger. The doctor created a dairy-free formula and sent it to Chicago. It was effective. Roy grew swiftly and had less digestive difficulties. However, because illness and disease plagued him his entire life, the lack of natural milk most certainly contributed to a weakened immune system.

As if dealing with an unwell infant wasn't stressful enough for Elias and Flora, there was also concern for Elias's mother, Mary. Unfortunately, she found it more impossible to maintain the family farm, and it was sold on March 15, 1894, to pay off the debts her husband left behind when he died three years previously. She quickly moved in with Elias's younger brother Kepple, who, at 29, owned his own cattle ranch. While Elias was at ease knowing that his mother was being cared for by the family, his father's death and the loss of the farm were undoubtedly a source of stress for him as he struggled to provide for his own family.

Because of Chicago's high unemployment rate, Elias was unable to find regular employment and instead resorted to something he could do that drew on his carpentry skills: he opted to continue manufacturing furniture for sale. Members in the community had seen some of his work and began to commission it. Elias built tables, chairs, closets, and some specialist pieces during the next few years. His work was so distinct and well-crafted that local furniture stores took note and began ordering pieces for their showrooms. At one point, at the World's Columbian Exposition, he was even commissioned to create some sculptures for the exposition. While a door had closed when he was laid off from the Jackson Park construction team, another had opened for him, one that was much more comfortable and delightful for Elias.

This happiness, however, did not last long. Elias soon caught the restless bug that had afflicted his family, and he realised he wanted to use his skills for more than just making furniture. He and Flora had had so much fun planning and erecting their house on Tripp that they decided to try their hand at building a few additional houses in the neighbourhood. The couple bought two sites down the road from their house to build residences on, 1141 and 1209 Tripp Avenue, which were both within walking distance of the family home at the corner of Tripp and Keeler. Over the next few years, Elias would construct two houses in the worker's cottage design with bay windows on the front, similar to his own. The extra bonus of indoor running water and sewage, which the Disneys had integrated into their own home, was the appeal for potential purchasers. Elias signed the paperwork for 1141 Tripp over to George Ramonberg, a 42-year-old German immigrant who shared the house with another married couple and a few borders, in addition to his wife and two daughters. Shortly after, Elias sold 1209 Trip to railway engineer Harvey Craigmile and his wife Ethel. Ramonberg, a millwright, and Craigmile were the very type of individuals Elias wanted to sell his houses to: honest, hardworking family men working in Chicago's expanding industrial sector.

Building homes in the neighbourhood meant Elias and Flora had become more involved in the life of the local community and were well-known to others who lived nearby. They joined the Hermosa Congregational Church, which convened a few blocks away from the Disney house at 1042 North Forty-third Avenue, shortly after Roy was born. It was led by Reverend H. W. Chamberlain, who increased the church's influence in the community. Chamberlain recognized the need for a new structure as the congregation increased and the church launched programs that drew more people from the surrounding area. A parcel at 2255 Forty-Second Avenue was identified, and a Building Committee was formed. Reverend Chamberlain was impressed by Elias' experience building homes in the neighbourhood and asked him to join the committee.

Chamberlain resigned from his position now that his mission to enhance the church's influence in Hermosa had been completed. He relocated to Honolulu, entrusting his flock to a young pastor named Dr. Walter R. Parr. Recognizing Elias and Flora's devotion and commitment to both the church and the community, Parr and his wife Mary immediately became friends with the Disneys, who were given greater roles in the church's life. Flora became the church treasurer and organist, while Elias became a deacon and occasionally filled in at the pulpit when Parr was away.

Parr and the Building Committee agreed it was time to start building the new church building in early 1900. With the relocation of the church, a new name was chosen. It was now known as St. Paul's Congregational Church. For the groundbreaking, an elaborate ceremony was planned to highlight the symbolism and significance of the church's role in the community. Reverend Parr arrived early on the day of the service, May 19, 1900. He started wandering around the parking lot, armed with a tape measure and wooden spikes, to mark off the external limits of the church structure. Around 5.00 p.m., members of the congregation, Sunday school, Christian Endeavor program, and other neighbourhood residents began to come, many carrying digging tools such as shovels, rakes, picks, and spades. As the ground-breaking began, several men joined their families, pulling their tiny children in wheelbarrows that would be used to cart away dirt. Elias and Flora stood next to Parr and his wife, greeting everyone who had come to help celebrate the event.

Small groups of people stood around conversing while waiting for the congregant who would bring the plough used in the ceremony to arrive. Jennie Bradshaw, a member of the church's Finance Committee, moved from group to group handing out little badges commemorating the event. Shaped like sickles, the badges labelled people at the ground-breaking as 'Reapers', with a reference to Luke 10:2 below, noting that 'the harvest is great but the labourers are few'. On the back of the badges, a question was put to the wearer: "Will you be one?"'

The plough arrived around 6 p.m., and several of the men got to work connecting a rope to the front. The congregation gathered around Reverend Parr, who was flanked by members of the Building Committee and church leadership. Following Parr's brief prayer, the church choir and orchestra joined the congregation in singing I Love Thy Church, O God. As the last note faded, the reverend cleared his throat and addressed the audience.

"Tonight we will commemorate this sacred ground for St. Paul's

Congregational Church," he went on to say. "This ceremony symbolises the united effort that has brought the church to its current strength and will make it even stronger and more useful in the future." The dragging of the plough through the soil by all members of the congregation pushing on the rope represents what the church will achieve in Hermosa and throughout Chicago. The church will fail to fulfil its objective unless the community of St. Paul's works together in the future."

Parr looked about at his flock of sheep and grabbed up the rope from the ground, holding it in the air. "I ask of you, men, women and children, to take hold of this rope as we break ground for this, our new church."

As more church members filed near the plough, a swarm of young boys dashed forward and grabbed the rope. The enthusiastic teenagers immediately began pulling on the rope, flipping the plough and dragging it across the field on its side. A couple men ran up to the boys and stopped them, one of them pushing ahead to reset the plough in its furrow. Recognizing the gravity of the situation, the boys' parents and other church members chose a space on the rope, sinking into a solemn state of devotion.

Reverend Parr took a position behind the plough, ready to take over the handles when the time came. Members of St. Paul's Building Committee Dr. H.J. Patton and John Ferrier tied themselves to the front of the plough as one would a horse. Ferrier joked with Patton that he would only "consent to be yoked in with the doctor on condition that the latter would not shy away from white bits of paper or get his feet mixed up in the traces." The small group of men laughed, including Elias, who hitched himself to the plough in front of Patton and Ferrier; Elias' yoke was attached to the rope that the congregants would pull.

"You're not going to flee, are you, Disney?"" Ferrier phoned.

The men laughed once again.

Reverend Parr gave the signal to his flock to begin pulling the rope as he pushed his hands down onto the handles of the plough after verifying with the three yoked men. As the scores began to tug on the rope, the farming implement jumped into the air. Parr tried unsuccessfully to wrestle the steel-bladed plough back into the earth. One of the members, John Keeney, noticed the reverend's distress and stopped the pulling. He picked up the plough and walked it back to its original furrow, showing Parr what he did wrong: instead of pulling down on the handles, Parr needed to pull up on them to guarantee that the blade cut the ground. The command was issued, and the church members began pulling the rope once more, with Ferrier, Patton, and Elias digging in their heels as the metaphorical workhorses.

As it became clear that this attempt to break ground for the new church building would be successful, the choir began leading the congregation in singing the Doxology. Residents stood in the street cheering and ringing their bicycle bells, while one member blew into a tin horn in jubilation. Reverend Parr handed over the plough to Keeney at the conclusion of the first furrow, admitting that he was "not a success as a ploughman." Joined by his wife and Flora, the reverend observed as Keeney and his congregation made four loops around the staked perimeter of the new church building.

The celebrants let go of the rope after the fourth pass, and the Building Committee unhitched themselves from the front of the plough. The plough was connected to a team of horses, and members of the church, including Parr, grabbed shovels and began digging out the furrows, emptying the dirt and sod into wheelbarrows. Work at 2255 Forty-Second Avenue lasted until after dark. After an hour of digging, the work was completed, which was followed by singing and refreshments. Parr dismissed his sheep after another word of prayer and encouragement.

Elias and Flora would become increasingly close to the Parrs over the next few months as a result of Elias's work on the Building Committee. Elias visited the building site practically daily while checking on the worksites of the houses he was building in the neighbourhood, and Parr frequently consulted his older buddy about construction and carpentry concerns.

When both Mary Parr and Flora announced that they were pregnant in early 1901, the couples got increasingly closer. Mary and her husband were overjoyed: the young couple was expecting their second child soon after Ilene, their 2-year-old daughter. Elias and Flora, on the other hand, were equally surprised: after Roy was born in 1893, they had no intention of having any more children. However, Elias immediately put his sentiments of disbelief aside in favour of excitement. On one of their visits, Elias and Parr struck an agreement: if their wives had sons, they would name them after one other.

At first, Reverend Walter Parr did not keep his half of the bargain. Mary had a second daughter, Bernice, who was named after her mother. Charles, the couple's first son, was born in 1902. The pastor didn't remember his arrangement with his friend until the Parrs' fourth child was born in 1904, when he gave the baby the middle name Elias.

But Elias remembered his pledge. Flora gave birth to a son in the upstairs bedroom of their Tripp Avenue house on December 5, 1901. Walter Elias Disney was his parents' name.

Chapter Four: Moral Oblivion

Elias required a secure job now that Flora and Elias were the parents of four boys ranging in age from a newborn to a 13-year-old. In addition to continuing to design and sell furniture to local showrooms, Elias realised he had a natural ability for woodworking. Elias chose to pursue his new trade after the success of his first two spec houses on Tripp. He would build several residences in the region during the next few years, including two one-and-a-half-story frame cottages at 1676 and 1678 North Costello Avenue, respectively.

Even though he was very busy with business, 1249 Tripp Avenue was also a hive of activity. Young Walter was a well-behaved baby who was also healthy; he didn't have the lactose sensitivity that his bigger brother Roy did as a newborn. Walter rapidly became the family's pride, adored by his mother and brothers. Roy was particularly fond of his younger brother, Walter, and was frequently seen pushing him in a stroller up and down Tripp Avenue. He not only lavished care on his brother, but he also occasionally bought toys and modest gifts for him with his own money.

Walter spent time with Flora and visited his father's construction sites while his elder brothers went to school at nearby Nixon Elementary School, which was only a few blocks away. Flora gave birth to her fifth and final child just a few days after his second birthday, on December 9, 1903. Ruth Flora Disney, the family's first daughter, had finally arrived.

Walter and Ruth became playmates when their older brothers were at school as they grew older. While Elias adored his children, he became more of a father figure to them.

His growing piety and devotion at St. Paul's Congregational drove him to be more morally rigorous with his family. Perhaps as a result of his extended family's vices and behaviours in Canada and Kansas when he was younger, Elias became apprehensive of the temptations that an increasingly racially and economically diverse Chicago provided. He resisted all vices, never consuming alcohol or smoking. He had learned the value of hard work and honesty as a child and wanted to instil the same values in his children.

If his sons crossed the line, his sternness often took the shape of revenge. Walter was stubborn even as a toddler. After committing a crime, he would frequently flee from his father, intelligent enough to place a piece of furniture, such as a chair in the dining room, between him and his father. When Elias tried to reason with Walter, he would argue back, resulting in a confrontation of wills. Unfortunately for the irritated father, these incidents frequently devolved into a game of keep-away, making it difficult for Elias to reach his kid and discipline him. Flora would often come to the rescue by snatching up her child and tormenting her husband to pull him out of his irritated mood.

However, Elias did not waste any time in enforcing discipline on his other boys. After disrespectful behaviours or failing to exhibit honesty and good character, Elias would send the offender up to his bedroom. Roy, in particular, remembered standing beside his room's window, which looked out into the backyard, watching Elias cut a switch off the apple tree in the back corner of the yard, before bringing the small branch upstairs to punish his son with a light, yet painful, beating on the backside. In another case, it was discovered one evening around the dinner table that Raymond had stolen transfers from a tram conductor on his way to school. Transfers permitted those who had paid to ride on a public transportation vehicle to get off and board another one to continue their journey without having to pay another fare. Raymond was promptly sent up to his bedroom to await Elias' punishment as a result of his failure to practise excellent, honest character.

Elias' disciplinary method was not unheard of at the time. In reality, many fathers and authority figures subscribed to the adage "spare the rod, spoil the child." Elias simply believed that punishing his sons was a method to strengthen their moral character, something he did out of love in the moment. As a contractor in the construction and carpentry industry, I had enough examples of what vice and an immoral city might do to a person.

While Chicago was undoubtedly a capitalist powerhouse, as seen by the scores of new advancements introduced, such as elevators, skyscrapers, electric lights, and horseless trams, many of these new technologies drew both immigrants and American migrants. This was exacerbated by the train's significant presence in the lakeside city: as of 1892, one-twentieth of all railroad mileage in the world terminated in Chicago. The railroads, which served as a means of import and export from the city, aided the rise of a variety of key industries, including meatpacking and steel and iron manufacturing. The manufacturers required low-wage labourers; these positions were frequently allocated for unskilled and immigrant workers, all of whom descended to Chicago.

Germans, Swedes, Italians, Poles, Irish, and Eastern Europeans all found jobs and a new life in America's second largest city, which swiftly became a cultural melting pot. While many of these newcomers stayed in the city centre near their places of employment, others were able to afford to relocate out to the suburbs, settling in areas such as Humboldt Park and Hermosa. The influx of people into Chicago caused the city to grow at an exponential rate throughout the Disneys' time there. Chicago had a population of about one million people when Flora and Elias arrived from Florida. When Walter was born ten years later, the population had nearly doubled. Chicago rapidly became congested, resulting in issues such as pollution, homelessness, and sickness. Corrupt politicians used immigrants' lack of understanding of the American political system, buying votes with promises of homes and jobs. By opening saloons, gambling houses, and brothels, enterprising business people took advantage of the greater population to cater to the needs and aspirations of stressed-out immigrants, while police officers received bribes to look the other way.

Saloons and brothels began to proliferate in middle-class society. Temperance organisations, which tried to reduce alcohol consumption, began to pop up across America, including major towns like Chicago. They claimed that any type of booze caused moral forgetfulness and had a negative impact on the family. When a husband consumes alcohol, he is wasting money that could be spent on his family. Alcohol consumption also functioned as a gateway to other hobbies and behaviours. A Drunkard's Progress, a popular political cartoon from earlier in the century, suggested that simply having a nice drink with an associate could escalate to violence, criminality, social ostracism, and, eventually, suicide. While this was certainly a skewed and exaggerated image intended to demonstrate the ills of vice and the potential repercussions it could have on the American family, the presence of alcohol did result in an increase in other activities regarded problematic and immoral by respectable' Chicago society. The level of organised crime has risen dramatically. Graft and political scheming became commonplace. Brothels arose in Chicago's red-light area, the Levee, catering to all strata of Chicago society. Many blamed the lack of morals that seemed to have taken over downtown on the region's enormous influx of immigrants.

Unfortunately, Elias began to believe that even his humble neighbourhood in Hermosa was not immune to the corruption and depravity in the downtown region, which was only a few miles away.

Many good Irish, Swedes, and Poles lived on Tripp Avenue, which had begun to attract immigrant families. They were now well-behaved, but God forbid they attracted more immoral or corrupted immigrants from the city's temptations.

Things became harsher and more 'hazardous' as more people moved to Hermosa. Elias became discouraged when saloons began to sprout up on street corners near the Disney estate. Unattended children and teenagers began to run around the neighbourhood. The concerned father contacted the local police, but despite promises to clean up the neighbourhood, nothing appeared to happen. In private, he complained to Flora that the cops were dishonest and undoubtedly took bribes to look the other way when mischief was committed.

This trend, however, was not limited to Hermosa. In the early twentieth century, Chicago was infamous for its prominent crimes and vices, which were frequently attributed to the city's large immigrant population, as well as severe congestion. Immigrants from Central and Eastern Europe travelled from New York to Chicago in search of work in the nation's largest industrial metropolis in the late nineteenth and early twentieth centuries. At the turn of the century, Chicago was home to a plethora of industrial and manufacturing occupations, including those in steel, meatpacking, railroad, and printing. The city's youth were difficult to contain in the city's public schools: those who weren't working in factories or selling newspapers on street corners frequently obtained street education in petty crime by spending time with other adolescents or unemployed adults. Many of the problems caused by the immigrant population were attributed to their inability to assimilate into American culture, according to reformer Jane Addams; in an effort to help these 'poor huddled masses,' she established Hull House, a settlement house that provided services such as Americanization classes and job training for new immigrants living in inner-city Chicago. Addams' efforts did not affect the nativist beliefs that many Americans had, particularly those who lived near immigrants. Stereotypes, bigotry, and racism persisted, as did scapegoating for the city's problems, further dividing native-born Americans and European immigrants.

In mid-1903, Elias Disney reached his breaking point in Chicago. On the evening of July 4, four young males aged 18 to 21 barged into the Chicago and Northwestern Railway's Clybourn Junction station and demanded money. One of the station's staffers, L.W. In the subsequent scuffle, Lathrop was shot, but the young men escaped with $70. A week later, the same young men went into a saloon. When the proprietor and a customer named Otto Bauder were told to raise their hands, Bauder ran. One of the teenagers shot him, and he died as a result of his injuries. This time, the gang made off with $50. Over the course of the next week, the young men robbed two additional saloons.

A few weeks later, on August 30, the young guys disguised themselves by wearing underwear on their heads and entered a street railway car barn near the intersection of Sixty-Fifth and State streets. Recognizing that some of the street railway staff were totaling up the day's fares, one of the thieves shot through the glass, while another rammed down the door with a sledgehammer. One of the shots struck Frank Stewart, and his two coworkers, William Edmund and Henry Biehl, were also severely hurt by stray gunfire. James Johnson, a fourth employee who had been sleeping in an adjoining room and had hurried to the murder scene, was also killed. One of the assassins snatched the mound of cash from the table where Stewart, Edmund, and Biehl were counting it and left with more than $2,500.

While the Chicago Police had dismissed the saloon robberies as the work of petty thieves, the car barn heist and killings made them painfully aware of what they were up against. Herman Schuettler, the captain of Chicago's Sheffield Avenue police station, began investigating the incidents and knew where he may find the car barn bandits from an informant.

Schuettler sent two of his investigators, John Quinn and William Blaul, to Greenberg's Saloon on Robey and Addison Streets in northwest Chicago, to apprehend one of the gang's members. When the detectives entered the saloon, they discovered a lone guy sitting at the bar with his back to them. He noticed the two detectives approaching him in the mirror across from him. He quickly turned back and retrieved a handgun from his pocket, shooting at the detectives and killing Quinn. When the young man attempted to shoot at the other detective, his revolver jammed; Blaul attacked the young man and held him to the ground until backup came, after which he was hauled down to the police station.

Gustave Marx was one of the four men responsible for a succession of saloon robberies in July and the car barn robbery and killings at the end of August. He promptly confessed to his crimes, implicating Peter Neidermeier, Harvey Van Dine, and Emil Roeski as his co-conspirators.

The other three perpetrators quickly learned of their friend's arrest and fled to Indiana, hoping to flee Chicago before being apprehended by the authorities. They took refuge in a dugout south of town, where they hid until they ran out of food in late November, when they slipped out to a nearby grocer. When Neidermeier withdrew a thick roll of dollar bills from his pocket to pay for their food, a schoolteacher, Henry Reichers, observed the lads. On closer inspection, he recognized the three young men from their newspaper descriptions and notified authorities, who swiftly deployed eight detectives to the site Reichers specified. When the investigators arrived, however, Neidermeier, Van Dine, and Roeski had already fled. Fortunately, new snow had fallen, and they were able to follow the trio's tracks to another nearby shelter. The investigators encircled the building and summoned the teenagers, but instead of complying, the young gangsters began firing their firearms at the detectives outside, killing one and injuring another.

The three young males were able to flee during the ensuing pandemonium. Van Dine, on the other hand, had been wounded in the cheek, while Roeski had been shot in the hip. Roeski left Neidermeier and Van Dine behind and continued to stagger 8 miles to nearby Aetna, where he could catch a train on the Wabash line out of Illinois. Van Dine and Neidermeier went into a nearby train that was parked at a station and ordered the engineer and brakeman to uncouple the engine from the rest of the carriages. The brakeman mistook Neidermeier for inebriation and grabbed his wrist to force the revolver away; he was instantly shot dead. This persuaded the engineer, who launched the engine down the rails, away from the chasing cops. However, one of the detectives had called the railway authorities ahead of time, and the train was diverted to a side track. The crooks instructed the engineer to reverse the engine until it was back on the main line, at which point they leaped off the train and fled across a cornfield.

A nearby group of farmers on a rabbit hunt heard the ruckus and joined in the chase as the police arrived at the stopped train. When they came to a halt in a frozen marsh, Neidermeier and Van Dine stacked up dead corn stalks to hide behind. This barricade was no match for the farmers, who fired their shotguns into the cornstalks; small rounds of buckshot injured the two young guys, who exchanged glances and stepped out from behind the stalks, hands outstretched.

"Don't shoot," said Harvey Van Dine. "We surrender." The farmers kept their weapons fixed on the murdering youngsters until the police arrived, led by railway secret service officer Captain William Briggs, who effected the arrest.

"We surrendered because you are not police and we want to see our mothers again," Neidermeier said to the farmers as he and his partner were carried away into the waiting police van.

The police arrived at the Aetna rail station a mile away, a few minutes before Van Dine and Neidermeier were apprehended. They had got information that a 'breathless man in his shirt sleeves and covered in blood' had entered a house and requested a coat. When he was refused, he went to the adjacent train station. After cleaning himself up in the restroom, the strange-acting young man fell asleep on a bench in the station's waiting room. When the cops arrived at the train station, Emil Roeski was sound asleep, weary by his escape and the blood loss from his hip wound.

Over the next few months, all four youngsters, who became known as 'The Car Barn Bandits' by the media, would face trials. On 22 April 1904, Peter Neidermeier, Harvey Van Dine, Gustav Marx, and Emil Roeski were all found guilty of various charges of murder, including the murder of two police officers, and condemned to death by hanging. However, Roeski's sentence was eventually commuted to life in prison at Joliet State Prison after it was found that he could not have fired the shot that killed Otto Bauder in the first heist on July 4th. In late November 1904, Rocky's brother, Herman, attempted to escape by transferring tools through the bars to Email. However, the plan was foiled, and Herman Roeski was sentenced alongside his brother.

Throughout 1903 and 1904, the narrative of the young gangsters dominated the news, as well as the thoughts and opinions of Chicago residents. A number of copycat gangs formed, composed of young men who carried out their own robberies and killings. This tendency continued during the early 1900s when the Chicago economy suffered a minor downturn, leading to an increase in crime. Unfortunately for Elias, this meant that the housing market dried up, putting him out of work once more.

Elias Disney was particularly concerned about the rise of boy gangs and their crimes. Many of the robberies and murders committed by Neidermeier and crew at the saloons took place less than three miles from the Disney home on Tripp Avenue. In fact, some gang members, like Emil Roeski, attended St. Paul's Congregational, the church where Elias and Flora served as deacon and treasurer, respectively. Because the boys were the same age as Herbert and Raymond, Elias was concerned about his kids' morality when he observed them spending time with the alleged killers.

Sophia Van Dine, the late young criminal's mother, authored a series of articles for The Chicago Tribune in February 1906 explaining why so many Chicago teenagers had joined gangs and turned to a life of vice, robbery, and murder. Mrs Van Dine had dedicated her life to assisting disturbed youngsters in the aftermath of her son's death at the hands of the law, seeking to prevent them from suffering a similar fate. She stated that it was "the responsibility of normal minded men and women" to help the delinquents, whom she referred to as "feeble-minded" and "developmentally dwarfed." She went on to say that many of these guys had been corrupted by their own fathers, who were either absent or prone to vice and violence, and lived a life of alcoholism or beat their wives and children, due to their inability to determine what was morally acceptable behaviour. She proposed isolation as a solution, removing these young men from the rest of society and thereby keeping them from a life of crime, as well as making it impossible for them to procreate and create 'maybe to a greater degree the flaws of the parents'.

What bothered Elias the most was Mrs Van Dine's argument in an article published on the morning of February 6th. She said that young men's underdeveloped minds prohibited them from recognizing the criminal defects of others around them. The city's youth congregated on street corners, in abandoned buildings and residences, and in saloons and pool halls. What started as vice and bad language evolved into petty theft before escalating into holdups, armed violence, and, eventually, murder. The prevalence of this crime in the area surrounding the Disney home on Tripp Avenue concerned the Disney patriarch: his two oldest sons, Herbert and Raymond, were the same age as the Car Barn Bandits when they began their rampage of crime, and had, on occasion, spent time with the boys through their association with the family's church.

Fearing that his kids would follow in the footsteps of other young men in the neighbourhood, Elias concluded that the temptations of city life were too much for his family. He was resolved to find a more rural setting where his children might understand what it means to live an honest, hardworking, and diligent life. While the transition from Big City Chicago to Main Street, USA would be significant for the Disney children, Walt would remember them fondly as some of the best years of his early life.

PART III: THINGS OF IMPORTANCE – MARCELINE, MISSOURI, 1906–1911

Chapter Five: Smalltown Folks

"Where are we going?""Elias thought to himself. The morality of America's cities had clearly deteriorated in the sixteen years they had lived in Chicago, with the rise of organised crime, prostitution, gambling, and alcoholism. This was hardly the milieu in which he had envisioned parenting four sons and a daughter.

The family patriarch reflected on his own adolescence spent working on farms in Canada and Kansas. He learned the value of determination, hard work, honesty, and community here. In an era of economic struggle following the recent crisis, he sought to instil these qualities in his young family.

Together, Elias and Flora began scouring rural America, contacting landowners, real estate agencies, and their extensive network of family and friends in search of possibilities to purchase farmland. While Steamboat Springs, Colorado and Citronella, Alabama were on their list, he chose to follow the counsel of his younger brother, Robert.

Robert Disney, a businessman, had been engaged in real estate speculation for many years. After leaving the family farm in Kansas, Robert was enticed by the potential of fortune in Chicago, which was competing to host the World's Columbian Exposition in 1893. Recognizing that hundreds of thousands of people would be visiting the Great White City to enjoy everything the fair had to offer, he put an ad in The Chicago Tribune in March 1892 offering to pay between $80 and $120 per square foot of land on Chicago's South Side for the purpose of constructing a hotel.

Robert began to explore elsewhere for a business opportunity that would enrich him, anticipating that the hotel business in Chicago would shrink after the exhibition. His attention was drawn to a land development opportunity near the shores of Lake Michigan, where he would get a deed of land in exchange for services rendered in place of money compensation from land 'developer' Captain George Wellington Streeter. Unfortunately for Robert, the land he got from Streeter, as well as surrounding acres, swiftly became the focus of one of Chicago's most contentious conflicts in the late nineteenth century.

In 1886, George Wellington Streeter, captain of the small boat Rutan, transported passengers between Chicago and Milwaukee. He came across a 1755 map that showed an area owned by the British and later the United States government under the rules of the Treaty of Paris' organisation of the Northwest Territory. Streeter realised that the area beneath Lake Michigan's surface was unclaimed territory. The skipper left the Rutan anchored offshore in a region of the lake used to dump rubbish and ashes near Superior Street in northern Chicago, waiting for a storm that would ruin the ship and allow him to carry out his plan. Fortunately for the con artist, a storm soon arrived, and the high waves of Lake Michigan grounded the small ship on a sandbar.

As debris from the storm began to be cleaned from Lake Michigan's shoreline over the next two weeks, Streeter skillfully positioned storm logs and tree branches between his grounded boat and the shore. As the currents flowed parallel to the shore, this blocked sand, as well as floating rubbish and deposited ashes, creating a dry channel. Streeter secured control of his artificial island and the increasing land around it by claiming squatters' rights, transforming the Rutan into a modest house and moving in with his wife.

As Captain Streeter's claim grew to 156 acres, he had it surveyed and platted into 1,900 prime lots for sale to those interested in owning property along the lakeshore, while earning $150 per month from those who chose to rent shanties rather than buy land outright. The captain was able to sell 300 lots, including some to Robert and Margaret Disney, earning more than $200,000 from property sales ahead of individuals with original claims to the beach, such as N.K. Fairbank approached local law enforcement to fight against Streeter's claims to the land and the sale of it.

To validate his claims, Streeter petitioned the US government to acquire the region, which he had established as the District of Lake Michigan. He gave the US four options: the area may be annexed as part of the state of Illinois, added to the territory of Alaska, founded as an entirely new state, or rejected by the US and become an autonomous entity comparable to Puerto Rico. To make his proposition more tempting, the captain established his own government, including treasurers and judges, and published his own constitution. One component of this founding document was particularly appealing: it granted citizenship and voting rights to all women aged 18 and older, which was not granted to American women until the Nineteenth Amendment to the United States Constitution. More than two decades later, the Constitution was ratified.

The United States and the state of Illinois both refused Streeter's offer, and in 1893, police forces were dispatched to the District of Lake Michigan, arresting the captain and demolishing the shanties that had been built along the coast. Even while in jail, the arrested guy insisted that the Chicago police were crooked and had been paid to arrest him, despite the fact that he had committed no crime. The Streeter saga was finally put to rest when the city of Chicago filled in the lake surrounding the District of Lake Michigan in order to develop Lincoln Park and Lake Shore Drive along the coast, effectively eliminating Streeter's claim to the land.

With the metropolis of Chicago virtually burying Robert's newest land development prospect, the investor went to Marceline, Missouri, a little village along the Santa Fe Railroad that was slowly becoming an important farming community. While the area was previously known as Bucksnort and consisted of privately held farms, the town of Marceline was formed as a division point along the railroad in 1888, named after the wife of one of the Santa Fe Route's directors. During the 1800s, railroads established waypoints every 160 kilometres for trains to refuel and resupply; Marceline was established as a prime location for the railroad's waypoint, which stretched between Chicago and Kansas City, Missouri, due to the prevalence of creeks flowing in the area, as well as the discovery of coal nearby. Recognizing the importance of gaining the support of the families who own farms in the Bucksnort area, the railroad corporation began to construct facilities to sustain the traffic that a waypoint along the Santa Fe would bring. Along the rails, a two-story wooden station with a dining hall and overnight rooms for train personnel was built. Following the discovery of coal, the Marceline Coal and Mining Company was formed, and Mine No. 1 was opened, providing a number of jobs for men in the area. The main routes through town were graded and paved, construction of a downtown began, and within a few years, a power plant a few hundred metres from the train station was built, giving electricity to the town.

However, in order for Marceline to thrive, it needed to attract families as well as men to work on the train line or in the coal mine. E.P. Ripley, president of the Atchison, Topeka & Santa Fe Railroad, recognized the need for outdoor recreation space and gave a few acres of property to the town for the creation of a park. Ripley Park, named in his honour, included a huge pond, green space, and a gazebo for community concerts and gatherings. The downtown area that grew along Kansas Avenue, the town's main street, quickly added an opera house, department store, banks, a school, boarding houses, and a hotel, all of which not only served those passing through town by train, but also those who lived near the mines or on nearby farms.

When Robert Disney learned that the Santa Fe line would be built through northern Missouri through his Chicago investor network, he purchased 400 acres of land and sold some of it to the Santa Fe Railroad, increasing the premium to make a profit for himself. He kept the remaining area northwest of downtown Marceline for himself, developing a row crop farm that mostly grew maize to be put onto trains at the local depot and shipped across the country. The enterprising investor, however, was not a rural boy: Robert and his wife Margaret lived in Kansas City, about 200 kilometres to the southwest, while local help managed the farm in his absence.

However, Robert and Margaret were not faraway investors out to make a quick buck off the labour of the locals. The couple frequently came to town, riding the Santa Fe and then switching to a horse-drawn buggy that transported them to their estate a few kilometres distant. It was evident to the inhabitants of Marceline that Robert and

Margaret were wealthy out-of-towners; Robert regularly roamed downtown in fine suits packed with accessories such as golden pocket napkins and watch chains, an expensive cigar hanging from his lips, earning him the nickname 'Gold Bug Disney'. However, recognizing the importance of the people of Marceline to the prosperity of his farm, as well as recalling his own small-town agricultural beginnings in Goderich and Ellis, Robert was sympathetic to those in town, aiding its citizens when he could.

As a result, when Elias remarked to Robert that he and Flora were seeking for a place to relocate their family that reflected their ideals of community and hard work, Robert enthusiastically proposed the small town of Marceline. When Elias agreed that Marceline would be ideal for his family, Robert bought the property of the recently deceased William Crane from Crane's wife, who had relocated to New York to be with family following her husband's death. Crane had obtained his acreage in northern Missouri as reward for his service in the 94th Infantry of New York during the American Civil War, and he had lived on it for twenty-seven years before his death. In turn, Robert Disney sold it to Elias for $125 per acre in order to ease his brother's family's relocation into town. The 45-acre property had a two-story white clapboard farmhouse, a modest red barn, animal cages and pastures, and fields of crops such as sorghum, corn, and two orchards growing Wolf River apple trees.

Elias was keen to relocate his family away from Chicago. He bought four train tickets for Flora, Roy, Walter, and Ruth and dispatched them to Marceline with a few of the family's goods to get settled on the farm. He, Herbert, and Raymond stayed in Chicago to settle their business before transporting the rest of the family's belongings via rail freight later.

As the train approached Marceline, plumes of steam emitted from the locomotive, forcing dust that had accumulated on the bricked train station to fly into the air in swirling clouds. Roy assisted his mother in loading the family's belongings onto a handcart on the platform. He and Flora each took one of the younger children's hands and stepped off the train into the shadow of Marceline's two-story wooden station for trains and passengers passing through town.

Flora explained to her children as they walked around to the front of the station that Mr James Coffman, a local citizen, would be collecting them up and delivering them to their new farm. Flora put on a brave face for her children, but she was inwardly anxious about her position as a mother rearing a young family on the farm, and she hoped she could fully arrange things before Elias and her two older sons arrived.

While it was an early spring day with moderate temperatures, the sun's beams beat down on the family, who were accustomed to wearing heavy and layered garments required for living in the north. Flora directed her children to a spot across the street from the station that was shaded by a massive grain elevator. Walter and Ruth linked hands as they followed their mother, with Roy close behind pulling the handcart filled with luggage.

The family didn't have to wait long, as an old horse clip-clopped along the bricked road, carrying a cart pulled by a grizzled guy approximately Elias's age. The man stopped the beast in front of the family. While Roy began to load the trunks and bags onto the back of the cart, the two adults chatted pleasantries. Mr Coffman assisted Flora onto the cart before lifting Walter and Ruth to their mother, who settled the two for the voyage to their new home. Young Walter was captivated by the rural landscape as the horse-drawn buggy slowly made its way north to the family's new home, a stark contrast to urban Chicago: Missouri's rolling green hills were crowned by bright blue skies, with alternating lots featuring houses, cattle pastures, and row crops on either side of the road.

The little farmhouse was ideal for the Disneys. A kitchen and parlour on the first floor served as the family's entertainment room. Herbert and Raymond occupied a small bedroom off the parlour because, at the ages of 17 and 15, they were frequently engaged labouring on the family farm as well as other farms in the region, and needed an accessible egress from the house at all hours of the day due to the nature of their work. The upper floor included three bedrooms, including a small room for Elias and Flora and two equally-sized rooms at the front of the home, one shared by Roy and Walter and another across the hall for Ruth alone, which she appreciated as the only girl in the family. While there was no power or running water when the Disneys moved in - Flora had to obtain water from a handpump in the kitchen - Elias insisted on having a telephone. Life in Chicago had taught him the advantages of evolving technologies, and he was always on the lookout for new chances, hoping to stay ahead of the curve and perhaps open lucrative doors for him. Elias was thrilled that his new home included closets in each of the bedrooms, recognizing the benefit of closets at the Tripp house in Chicago. He was willing to pay a little more for a house with closets (additional rooms resulted in higher taxes on a house than those without). The family did, however, miss having a restroom, especially during the winter months. Unlike their Chicago home, which had a small water closet behind the stairs, the Marceline farmhouse had an outhouse located a distance away from the house to protect the water supply from contamination.

While Flora worked on getting things settled at the farmhouse over the next few weeks, Elias finished up in Chicago. The sale of his and his wife's Tripp family home was completed, and the deed was given to a young family of German immigrants who had lately come to Hermosa. Raymond and Herbert assisted their father in packing up the family's goods and selecting a team of draught horses at the city stockyards before loading everything onto a boxcar and taking the Santa Fe to Marceline.

For the Disneys, life in a small, rural village was very different. The five children, aged three to seventeen, undoubtedly learnt the values their father hoped to instil in them through living in an agricultural village, rather than those learned in the big city. Marceline, with a population of only 5,000 people, had a strong feeling of community, which was reflected by the interdependence that existed among its residents.

Elias rapidly immersed his family in the activities of the town, remembering the importance of neighbours to one's survival from his time in Ellis. Many of the residents who had arrived from Europe to work in the coal mines spent their leisure time playing instruments because it was a low-cost pastime. These musical coal miners formed bands, such as the Marceline Town Band, to perform at Ripley Park's gazebo on weekends. Over time, the band grew to include men who worked on surrounding fields and for the Santa Fe Railroad, and Elias soon added his fiddling talent to these concerts. Neighbours also frequently assisted one another in annual agricultural activities such as barn raising and harvesting. Fathers who owned their own farms or worked in the region's other major industries frequently hired out their children to the town's farmers to help with work; for example, both Herbert and Raymond worked on threshing crews on a number of farms, including the Disney farm and the Taylor farm, located just down the road.

Even young Walter, at the age of six, was required to help with agricultural labour: when he wasn't riding a horse around a millstone to crush sorghum on his father's farm, he was paired up with a neighbour youngster, Patrick Shermuly, to deliver water to those working on the threshing crews. However, young Walter was uninterested in his job. Like one of his literary heroes, Tom Sawyer, the child frequently persuaded others to take on more responsibilities so he could sit back and relax. On the Disney farm, Walter was also in charge of herding pigs. When he saw the animals were recalcitrant and refused to move in the direction he intended, he mounted the back of one of the largest sows, Porker, and rode it like a horse to persuade the rest of the hogs to move towards the pen. This didn't exactly work out as planned: the sow proceeded towards the farm's muddy pond and reared, sending Walt into the mud. While his plans to herd the pigs had failed, the child had acquired a new hobby, choosing to play with the cattle over the responsibilities assigned to him by his father.

Walter's tasks of caring for the farm's animals resulted in his building wonderful relationships with the animals. Porker flung the child off her back and into the mud whenever he tried to ride her, but she recognized him as one of her regular playmates. When Walter and Ruth had chickenpox, Porker came up onto the farmhouse porch and started oinking and pawing at the front door. Flora went upstairs to Walter and Roy's room, where the sick young boy was resting in bed, after keeping an eye on Ruth as she sat against the vent of the stove, where the heat could assist break her fever. Walter smiled as he saw his heavy friend was ready to play on the porch.

Walter also had feelings for a little piglet named Skinny. The piglet was the runt and couldn't get through the pack of his siblings and sisters to feed at his mother, so Walter, feeling sorry for the critter, started feeding it with a bottle. The child and piglet formed a bond, and the piglet began to follow Walter around the farm like a puppy.

Living in a small farming town also meant getting to know your neighbours quickly. Across the street from the Disney farm lived Erastus Taylor and his wife, Elizabeth, who were affectionately referred to as 'Grandpa Taylor' by everyone in town. The Taylors were one of Marceline's founding families, purchasing land from the Burlington Railroad in 1867, more than two decades before the town was incorporated. Taylor was also instrumental in the creation of the town, contributing property for the area's first cemetery and constructing the town's first school, where he taught in addition to farming his 80 acres of land.

The Taylor property's proximity to William Crane's farm reflected the essence of small-town life: Crane's niece, Bertha Phillips, had married Erastus's son, Manly Howe Taylor. Erastus Taylor was also boyhood friends with Crane's brother-in-law, Bertha's father, Josiah Phillips. As a result, while Erastus and William Crane were not related, the connection between their families produced a kinship on which they learnt to rely. As a result, when Elias and his family relocated to the old Crane property, the Disneys became a part of the Crane/Taylor microcosm north of Marceline.

Young Walter spent considerable time across the street at Grandpa Taylor's house throughout the next few years. During the American Civil War, the old man enjoyed telling stories about his exploits as a private in Company H of the 6th Regiment of Minnesota Volunteers. Crane enrolled in February 1864 and was sent to Fort Ridgely in southwest Minnesota. Union troops were stationed there to protect the fort from Native Americans who had attacked it a few years before. The regiment travelled south to Helena, Arkansas, in June, and took over the previously held Confederate state. Warmer weather in Arkansas triggered a smallpox outbreak that killed 165 commanders and troops in Minnesota's 6th Regiment. Erastus became ill and was sent to Jefferson Barracks in St. Louis, Missouri, where he remained until May 1865, missing the Confederate surrender and the end of the war. His service was utilised to ensure Union occupation of the south after he was freed from the hospital, before he was discharged from US military service a few months later on 19 August 1865.

While Grandpa Taylor's accounts of 'his experiences' in the Civil War captivated young Walter's imagination, the kid soon realised that the old man could not have fought in every battle or met every general that he mentioned. However, the importance of Taylor containing vivid details and colourful people was not lost on Walter, who recognized the importance of Taylor including vivid details and colourful characters.

Manly Howe Taylor, Erastus's son, resided with his wife and five children around one kilometre west of the Disney farm, on the farm that Josiah Phillips had constructed following his arrival in Bucksnort more than twenty years before. Manly Howe's children were roughly the same age as the Disneys', giving Walter and Ruth quick playmates as well as new peers for Raymond, Herbert, and Roy. The Disneys also became close friends with the Flickingers and Rensimers, whose little kids, Clem and Will, were good friends with Walter and Roy.

But having pals wasn't everything to the older Disney lads. They had the opportunity to court country girls and farmers' daughters because they lived in a small midwestern agricultural village. Roy, in particular, had fallen for Fleta Rogers, who was discouraged from marrying as a teacher in one of the local schools. As a result, her desire in a romantic relationship with Roy was more casual than serious. While Rogers enjoyed spending time with Roy because he was a "nice boy," she had an evident crush on his elder brother Raymond and made every effort to catch his attention. Because Fleta's family lived on the main street downtown, she and her friends, dressed to the nines and with perfectly coiffed hair, would frequently sit on the front porch on Saturday nights waiting for Herbert and Raymond, who frequently attend social events in town. The girls would hurry to the porch balcony and call to the boys as the two brothers strolled past in their elegant suit coats, white flannel trousers, and tall straw hats. The two eldest Disneys would come to a halt and lean on the gate leading into the Rogers' yard, making small talk and occasionally making a polite but flirty comment to the girls. They would gently tip their hats to the young women, say good evening to them, and proceed on their way after a few minutes. Miss Fleta Rogers would invariably collapse onto the porch swing, flushed and breathless, knowing that Raymond Disney had noticed and spoken to her.

Fleta Rogers wasn't the only lady in town vying for his attention: 17-year-old Raymond was a ladies' man who frequently utilised his sophisticated charm to win dates with the local girls. Ray frequently brought them dancing or to the Ripley Park pond's banks. However, his casual manner with the girls only piqued their interest for a short time before they realised he wasn't interested in commitment and moved on to more steady men.

Physical distance and transportation constraints were not an issue for the Disneys' extended family during their stay in Marceline. The town's location along the Santa Fe Railroad actually made it easier for members of the Disney family to visit on occasion.

Walter was frequently indulged by his visiting family because he was the youngest. One example is when Elias's mother, Grandma Mary Richardson Disney, came to town to visit. Walter and Grandma Mary were like-minded in that they both enjoyed causing mischief, which Mary took advantage of. Mary took the youngster into town during one of her many visits to Marceline, walking around the country roads in the nice weather. Mary spotted some turnips that looked really good as they passed a tiny house with a garden in the front yard.

"Walter, crawl under that fence and fetch me some turnips," she told him. Eager to please his favourite grandmother, the child climbed into the garden and dug up the turnips the woman had indicated. Scrambling back under the fence, he passed the dirt-covered vegetables to Mary, who quickly wrapped them in her apron, not only to help carry them home, but also to conceal them from prying eyes.

When Walter and Mary returned home, they discovered Elias in the kitchen. Walter brags to his father about his achievement in getting the turnips for his grandmother. Elias was silent for a little moment. His face became increasingly redder as he frowned. Elias, looking down at his small son, began to teach him that stealing was ethically and religiously wrong.

"Thou shalt not steal," said the father.

"Oh, Elias, stop," his mother snapped. Her son's gaze shifted from the child to the elderly mother. "You're making such a big deal out of a few turnips." They had a lot more. There's no need to get so worked up." Mary turned and walked out of the kitchen, leaving her son considerably furious.

Mary led the boy into the front parlour, where she took out a small tin pillbox and extracted a round, red pellet. Walter adored these tasty pellets that melted in his mouth. The youngster made an effort to accomplish things for Grandma Mary in order for her to thank him with these delectable treats.

Flora happened to be in the room one day while Mary was rewarding her grandson with one of the pellets and, appalled, admonished her mother-in-law for giving the youngster the tablet. Walter had assumed he was being rewarded with sweets, but it turned out that his grandma was giving him Cascarettes, a popular patent laxative coated in sugar to make the medicine easier to swallow. Grandma Mary justified herself, claiming that giving her grandson laxatives not only encouraged the boy's excellent behaviour, but they may also help his digestion.

Grandma Disney didn't always solicit the help of her grandkids in causing mischief. She was also a very affectionate and nurturing person. Every evening during her stay, while Flora was cleaning up after dinner and Elias went out to finish the evening farm chores, Mary would take a volume of Grimm's Fairy Tales or Hans Christian Andersen stories from the fireplace mantle and sit on the floor with Roy, Walter, and Ruth. She would passionately spin tales for the next several minutes, occasionally utilising voices and acting out sections of the story, enthralling her grandchildren. Walter, Roy, and Ruth were so taken with this evening ritual that Flora continued it when Grandma Disney came home, but not as energetically as her mother-in-law.

Others drove the train into Marceline while some Disney relatives rode the train into town. Uncle Mike Martin, who was married to Flora's older sister Alice, worked as a locomotive engineer on the Atchison, Topeka & Santa Fe Railroad, primarily between Fort Madison, Iowa and Kansas City, Missouri. Martin would blast a distinct pattern on the locomotive's whistle as he reached Marceline on his route to Kansas City to notify his sister- and brother-in-law and their children that he was in town. Walter was attracted by trains as a young boy growing up in a railroad town and ran about 1.5 kilometres east where the Santa Fe crossed a railroad trestle. The small kid struggled up the rough hill where his uncle's train was waiting, and the sooty engineer would sweep up his nephew into the train's cab. Young Walter Disney would sit on his uncle's lap, tooting the train's whistle the last few kilometres into town before it halted at the Marceline station to be refilled before continuing south to Kansas City.

It took time to unload passengers and freight from Uncle Mike's train and replenish its stockpiles of coal, sand, and water for the next stage of its voyage. Rather than loitering in the train yard or eating at the train station's café, Martin would hitch a ride to the Disney farm, where Flora and Elias awaited him with a refreshing drink. The adults sat on the porch swing, while Walter and Roy sat on the porch steps with a paper bag of hard candies their uncle had bought them and listened to Uncle Mike and Elias spin tales about their time driving for and building the railroad, respectively. Elias told his kids that while he was building the Union Pacific, Buffalo Bill Cody, who later became famous for founding a Western-themed circus, would slaughter buffalo to provide meat for Elias' construction team. Uncle Mike also liked to tell the boys stories about important Civil War battles, as well as Casey Jones, an American tall tale based on a real-life railroad engineer named Jonathan Luther Jones, who had died a few years before when the passenger train he was driving collided with the rear of a freight train in Mississippi. Jones was well-known for his valiant but unsuccessful attempt to stop his train prior to the catastrophic disaster, earning his way into American legend for slowing the train from 121 kilometres per hour to 51, saving the lives of everyone else onboard.

If Mike Martin's stories and work aboard the Atchison, Topeka & Santa Fe Railroad can be attributed to Walter's lifelong love of railroads, another close family member is accountable for establishing an interest in art in the kid. Uncle Robert and his wife, Aunt Margaret, came to Marceline frequently, not only to see his brother, but also to check on his land, which was 4 kilometres west of Elias' farm. Margaret once brought her nephew a Big Chief tablet of paper and a box of crayons. Throughout her stay, she would frequently discover the boy in the parlour on his stomach, painting pictures of people and animals. whereas she pampered the boy to boost his self-esteem, many of her praises on his artwork were genuine; whereas many children his age were painting stick figures, the young artist was focusing on a more realistic and natural form.

Aunt Margaret's positive praise encouraged the child to keep drawing when he wasn't needed to help on Elias' farm. Walter had the opportunity to draw and enhance his depiction of people because he was part of a large family. However, like any obsessive reader, the aspiring artist began to seek out other sources of inspiration, such as commercials and newspapers. Elias read The Appeal to Reason, a weekly socialist periodical from Girard, Kansas. Flipping through the paper, the child noticed that it had political cartoons as well as usual comic strips, which he used to create new models.

Walter also drew his favourite animals from his childhood on his father's farm, including Skinny, Porker, and Martha (a hen). Elias made it clear that drawing was a hobby that would take place only in the boy's leisure time and would not interfere with farm tasks. Walter followed his father's orders, but it didn't keep him out of trouble. Walter and Ruth were strolling around the property one day, while Elias, Flora, and Roy had taken the buggy into town with a load of apples to sell and Herbert and Raymond were off working in the fields, when they stumbled across a barrel against the north side of the house. When the curious siblings opened the barrel's top, they discovered it was filled of black pitch.

Walter took a stick from the ground and inserted it into the barrel, inspecting the pitch that had been left on the tip.

"Oh!" shouted him. "This would be fantastic for painting with!"" The boy glanced around for a suitable surface to paint on, but nothing came to mind. Deflated, the boy gazed longingly back at the barrel and spotted the farmhouse's broad exterior wall covered in white clapboard siding. "Ruth, let's paint on the house."

"Will it fall off?"" Ruth inquired. "I don't think father will be very happy."

"Sure, it will come off," her older brother jokes. "Get a stick."

The ambitious artist dipped his makeshift paintbrush into the tar and began drawing images on the side of the home as the small girl picked up a stick from beneath a nearby tree. For the following few minutes, he imagined a world full of houses with smoke issuing from the chimneys and small, happy individuals standing close on the blank wooden canvas. Ruth, who was two years younger than her brother, drew zigzags beneath and beside the boy's town. After a while, the siblings took a step back from their creations, sticks in hand, to appreciate their work in the warm sunlight.

"We should probably start cleaning up before Mother and Father get back," he said. Ruth dashed inside to get a rag to scrub their work, but the tar had begun to set and harden and was no longer coming off the clapboard siding. When they heard the sound of hooves coming up the road, they were still trying to scrape the tar off the house. Walter felt a surge of terror as he peered around the corner of the house and saw his father, mother, and brother riding in the buggy past the front of the farmhouse. The child would be unable to conceal his labour from his father because the barn where the family stabled the horses and stored the buggies was on the property's northern edge.

When Elias discovered what his two youngest children had been up to, he was furious. He marched inside the house, snatching his own stick from the ground and disciplining both of his children. Walter's father grew agitated over the next few days when he realised he couldn't scrub or chip the tar drawings off the exterior of the house. He eventually gave in, assuming that others in town wouldn't see his children's labour because it was on the north side of the home.

To avoid a repeat occurrence, Elias advised his kid to bring his Big Chief sketching pad into the farmyard if he wished to draw outside. When he got weary of drawing his father's livestock, Walter would take his art equipment to surrounding farms and draw the animals of his neighbours. The youngster would lie on his stomach in the grass or perch himself on a fencepost. The young artist particularly enjoyed sketching a chestnut-coloured Morgan stallion who gracefully grazed in the pasture at one farm.

A shadow descended over Walter one day when he was painting the muscular horse, and the child started as he felt a strong touch on his shoulder. He turned around to see the farm's owner, Leighton Sherwood, standing behind him. While Sherwood was now a farmer north of Marceline, he had spent his career as a physician in the American Midwest, earning him the nickname 'Doc' in town.

"Not bad, Walter," the elderly man murmured, a smile growing across his naked, ruddy-complexion face as he looked over the artwork.

"Do you really enjoy it?"" The boy inquired.

"I sure do," Sherwood replied. His smile faded as a thoughtful expression crossed his face. "Say, you're not interested in selling that picture, are you?" Ole Rupert is my favourite horse, and I would love to own it."

Walter, the young man, was astounded. "Should I sell it?" You are welcome to it!"

Doc, on the other hand, merely shook his head, drawing the boy's hand toward him and placing a shiny quarter in his palm. Walter clambered down the fence after a brief conversation with the farmer, tucked his drawing pad under his arm, and rushed home clutching the quarter in his hand. He felt a small bulge in his pocket that he'd forgotten about: a buckeye that he took with him everywhere he went since his friends said it brought good luck. Perhaps his pals were correct.

It was the first time Walter Disney was paid for his artwork, but it would not be the last.

Chapter Six: Country Boy

While his childhood in Marceline, Missouri surely influenced Walter Disney's love of trains and his career path as an artist, it also instilled a sense of nostalgia, community, and small-town Americana that would later be embodied in his animated shorts, films, and theme parks.

Walter began to spend as much time as possible around the railroad and train yard after hearing Uncle Mike's stories of life on the Santa Fe Railroad and riding on his uncle's lap in the locomotive. He, Roy, and some of the boys from neighbouring farms, including Clem Flickinger and Don Taylor, would rush down to the railroad tracks and walk up and down the track, balancing on the steel rails. They would lie down on their bellies in the gravel or on the wooden ties at times, listening for vibrations from an incoming train. The neighbouring railroad trestles became a playground for the boys, who enjoyed climbing up and lounging across the wooden support beams while watching a train pass overhead. Walter and Roy would sneak down to the rail yards south of town on bright days, where sand and coal chutes towered over the engines being serviced. When no one was present, the lads climbed up the ladders that ran along the sides of the chutes and stood in the small shelters perched atop the buildings, observing the countryside and town.

Clem and Don were hanging out at the trainyards one afternoon in 1909 when they stumbled across a train being serviced before beginning its voyage down the Santa Fe. Don and Clem saw their friend didn't appear to be afraid of anything and was always up for adventure and taking risks, so they challenged Walter to blow the train whistle. He waited in the shadows of a nearby building until the engineer and trainmen had left, then climbed into the locomotive's cab. The adventurous child could view the area around him from his elevated position above the tracks in case the engineer returned, but the rumbling and hissing sounds emerging from the idling steam engine muffled any potential crunching of gravel if an adult made his way back to the train. Looking across at his companions who were still hiding, he smiled silly and went for the whistle's cord. After a little pause, he realised he still had the option to withdraw. Walter Disney, on the other hand, did not give up. The locomotive sent out a long, piercing whistle as he yanked on the cord. The child jumped from the train and onto the gravel without waiting to see how the trainyard staff reacted. As soon as his feet touched the earth, he dashed to where Clem and Don were hiding, and the three lads made their way back into downtown Marceline, giggling and yelling.

Walter's antics while spending time along the tracks and in the trainyard were not an exceptional incident among the Marceline boys: practically every young boy intended to work for the railroad when he grew up. Because the town was so vital to the operation of the Santa Fe Railroad, the lives of its residents and the local economy revolved upon providing goods and services that either serviced or profited from the trains passing through.

The slagheap at Coal Mine No. 1 of the Marceline Coal and Mining Company was another local hangout for Marceline adolescents, including Walter and his buddies. While there were several mines on the outskirts of town, the No. 1 mine was the closest to the Disney farm. Walter would frequently recline in his bedroom window seat, peering over the roof of Grandpa Taylor's house across the street, where he could see the top of the slagheap and mineshaft in the distance. It quickly became a figment of his imagination, and he privately claimed it as his personal mountain. He was willing to share 'his mountain' with others; he and Clem spent many summer afternoons climbing the slagheap, and on one occasion they even got to ride the elevator down into the mine, the cool underground air embracing the sweaty boys seeking relief from the dry midwestern summer heat.

An adventurous young Walter Disney had numerous possibilities growing up in a small rural Missouri community. Clem Flickinger's father would hook up his buggy on special occasions and drive Walter and his pals out to the nearby Yellow Creek, some 5 kilometres west of the Disney property, where they would spend the day fishing and swimming. Walter spent many of his summer days in Marceline here, catching catfish and bowheads from the wooden bridge, having picnics on the banks of the stream, and even stripping naked to bathe in the water with his pals. In the winter, many of the neighbouring children would venture out to skate on the frozen ice until dark, when someone would light a bonfire to keep the group warm as they trekked back to their different homes.

Walter would find his own pleasure closer to home on days when he knew his father expected him to work on the farm. On particularly hot days, after working in the sun for hours, he would sprint across the field to a grove of trees on the southwest border of the property, where a soaring 20-year-old cottonwood tree stood. The young dreamer would lie among the long grasses at its base, watching the meadowlarks, woodpeckers, and swallows flitting in the tree's fields and branches. The child also began to observe the numerous insects that scurried around the tree's trunk and among the roots coming out of the ground, bringing his Aunt Margaret's Big Chief drawing pad with him to sketch the critters. The cottonwood became known as his "Dreaming Tree," and his wildlife studies were known as "Belly Botany." Ruth would frequently accompany her older brother to his Dreaming Tree, where they would sprint around the trunk, climb high into the branches, and lie in the grass watching the clouds race overhead.

When he wasn't alone beneath his Dreaming Tree, the child was mixing his mischievous spirit with his imagination to develop a new trait: becoming a performer. Walter and Ruth discovered some burlap bags while crawling in the lofts of the barn north of the farmhouse one afternoon. When they looked closer, they discovered a barn cat inside, which had escaped from its hiding place when the youngsters approached. But this sight inspired the youngster: *What if he created a tent from this burlap bag for the barn cats to live in? This tent could be shaped almost like a circus tent. Wouldn't an animal circus be funny? What if he dressed up the farm animals as circus performers and charged his friends to see a show?*

So the boy got to work, cutting the burlap sacks apart and sewing them together, holding the interior up with sticks like a little circus tent. He searched his and Ruth's dresser drawers, removing those items he thought would look the most amusing on the animals, and dressed some up before putting them in a corral in the barn. Walter and Ruth ran around the local fields, gathering their friends and advertising a 'Disney Circus' performance later that day. When their pals arrived at the allotted time, Walter collected the 'entrance' fee of ten cents from each one before seating them in the grass in front of the barn door. Walter was bringing the barn cats, dogs, and even pigs out of the structure a few minutes later, dressed in his shirts and Ruth's gowns.

"What kind of circus is this?" Clem Flickinger yelled. "You can't teach a cat much of anything!"

Flora heard the commotion from the house and went to the barn, putting an end to her son's performance. She demanded that the ambitious showman refund his friends' money and that Walter and Ruth remove their garments from the animals. Flora, who has a penchant for humour and mischief, would have had a slight smile on her lips as she turned around to return to the farmhouse.

Life in a turn-of-the-century town also opened up new avenues for socialising and pleasure. Downtown Marceline had a number of individually owned businesses, including jewellers, restaurants, and department stores, as well as banks and theatres, throughout the first decade of the twentieth century.

As motion pictures and live theatre became more popular, tiny theatres began to open in Marceline to provide amusement for working- and middle-class families and people. Marceline had two theatres and an opera house by the time the Disney family left town in 1911. The Disneys occasionally took advantage of these entertainment possibilities, and it was the wonder of these performances that motivated the young Walter Disney to seek a career in the arts. Carter's Opera House, owned and managed by local businessman Dr. R.M. Cater, was located at the intersection of Kansas Avenue and Howell Street and featured travelling vaudeville troupes and shows supported by a small orchestra.

Young Walter saw his first live theatre performance at Carter's, a staging of Peter Pan. He was so anxious to watch the concert that had been advertised on plastered broadsides around downtown Marceline for several weeks that he decided to raid his piggy bank for enough coin to pay for his own admission. Maude Adams, one of America's most well-known theatrical actresses, played Peter Pan for the first time on Broadway in 1905. The play's success in New York prompted a national off-Broadway tour, which included a brief stay in Marceline. The youngster sat on the edge of his seat during the confrontations between Peter Pan and Captain Hook, and he enthusiastically engaged when Adams asked the audience to clap in unison in order to resurrect an unconscious Tinker Bell. The immersion of the audience in the plot and the attention to detail in a fantasy world piqued the boy's curiosity and led to his happy memories of the presentation years later.

The nickel theatres in Marceline also supplied a variety of diversions to the rural town's population, including the majority of the area's children. These theatres programmed films rented from distributors, such as adaptations of historical events and major works of literature. The Aerodrome, one of the town's theatres, was housed in a small storefront and played films projected on a bedsheet to viewers sitting in folding chairs. After being excused from school one day in 1910, 8-year-old Walter persuaded 6-year-old Ruth to accompany him to the movies on their way home, paying for her ticket. The program was a "Passion Film," representing episodes from Christ's life, crucifixion, and resurrection. Walter was entranced by the black and white images flying across the screen, oblivious to the sound of the film zipping through the projector in the rear of the room, much as he had been by Peter Pan. Walter and Ruth departed the theatre along Kansas Avenue after the brief film concluded. Walter initially thought his eyes were struggling to acclimate to the darkness of the Aerodrome over the previous 20 minutes. However, he soon realised that it had grown dark and that the lighting had turned on across Marceline's downtown. Walter grasped Ruth's hand and the siblings walked home together, apprehensive about the punishment their father would impose for their delay. After their 2.25-kilometer trip home, the kids discovered Elias and Flora relieved rather than angry, having avoided punishment for their violation - this time.

On rare occasions, the entire family would travel south to spend an evening in town. Elias invited his wife and children to a supper at the newly-opened Allen Hotel, which is located at the intersection of Kansas Avenue and Ritchie Avenue, south of Ripley Park. While the hotel mainly catered to guests arriving by train, a modest restaurant off the lobby provided meals to both visitors and locals. When the economic life of a farming family was unpredictable, eating at a restaurant was a rare luxury, but Elias was able to gather enough money to enjoy an evening at the Allen with the family. Everything was going swimmingly until Ruth collided with the table, spilling her plate of food all over her lap and onto the floor.

"Consarnit, Ruth!" Elias pronounced a curse. His oldest sons snorted; their father's property forbade him from swearing, so he invented his own curses. However, Elias was unaware of his sons. He was too preoccupied with the screaming girl in the chair across from him and the fact that the spilled meal was a waste of his money because the restaurant refused to replace the food that was now all over the floor and soiled his daughter's outfit.

Flora, on the other hand, stitched clothes for her children and could easily replace the destroyed outfit. When she wanted something more specialised than she could make, she went to Murray's Department Store on Kansas Avenue, just around the corner from the Allen Hotel. Flora frequently took Walter to Murray's, Marceline's largest department and dry goods store, where she bought him a pair of overalls to wear while working on the Disney farm.

The family's life in Chicago had been burdened with crime, vice, loudness, filth, overcrowding, and an oversupply of enterprises and services that had the potential to spoil and complicate life. However, life proceeded at a considerably slower pace in Marceline, providing opportunity for personal growth and greater awareness of the things - and people - that mattered.

Because of the small-town environment, neighbours became an extension of one's family, resulting in spending weekends and holidays together. After Ruth returned from the ladies' Sunday School class at Marceline's First Baptist Church, Elias and Flora would load the children into the buggy and drive a kilometre west to

Manly Howe Taylor's farm. There, the two families, joined by the Rensimer family, would spend the afternoon eating and performing music together. Will Rensimer and Elias played their violins, Ches Rensimer played the mandolin, and Winifred Taylor played the piano as the three families relaxed and enjoyed an afternoon of hymns, folk tunes, and classical pieces. The smaller children (Walter, Ruth, and Ken Taylor) were expected to sit quietly in the corner and listen to the others play music and sing, as both Elias and Manly Howe believed that Sunday was for relaxation and not play. The youngsters became restless and squirmy as the afternoons proceeded, and Bertha Taylor and Flora eventually allowed them to play calm indoor games like Old Maid and mumble-peg.

Neighbours were also brought together via community organisations. Several ladies from Marceline and its surrounding rural areas formed the Rural Home Circle, a social society in which members read poetry, sew and quilt together, organise events, and debate community issues. Flora joined her friends and neighbours, Bertha Taylor and her daughter Winifred, as well as Grandpa Taylor's wife, Elizabeth, and Emma Phillips, sister of the late William Crane, for the Rural Home Circle's regular meetings.

At the turn of the twentieth century, community was critical to the development of small agricultural towns across America. Crops would not have been harvested, barns would not have been built, and families would have lived in relative isolation if neighbours had not banded together. Instead, because midwestern agricultural towns are made up of migrants from all over the country, neighbours rapidly became adopted members of one's family, resulting in an extended network of honour, respect, and the sharing of talents and time.

While Walter Disney was born in Chicago and spent his first five years there, the importance Marceline and its people played in his childhood remained with him for the rest of his life: he considered Marceline, not Chicago, to be his hometown. Years later, during a ceremony in Marceline, he told a group of students that "my best memories are the years I spent here." You are fortunate to live here, children."

The trees he climbed, the animals he played with, and the duties he accomplished were not as important to the young Walter Disney. The neighbourhood - the places and people - had such an impact on the boy's life.

Chapter Seven: Hard Knocks

As the first decade of the twentieth century drew to an end, the hard times that often accompany farming finally caught up with the Disneys. While similar problems had been plaguing farmers west of the Mississippi for years, Elias' experience working with labour unions at the World's Fair in Chicago made the situation feel more personal. Elias Disney considered himself a follower of Eugene Debs and American socialism, as well as William Jennings Bryan, an advocate of Prairie Populism, which sought to improve conditions for farmers who had been victimised by the banking system and railroads and ignored by the federal government.

Land concessions began to be issued or sold to persons seeking new economic prospects in the days following the American Civil War, as the Transcontinental Railroad began its journey to the west coast of North America. While hundreds took advantage of the land provided by the United States government under the Homestead Act, others, notably immigrants such as Kepple and Mary Disney, purchased acreage offered for fundraising purposes by the different railroad lines developing in the west. While some farmers existed in the Marceline area previous to 1888, when the Atchison, Topeka & Santa Fe Railroad built the town as a division point, it drew an influx of people wanting to buy cheap land from the railroad to start their own farms.

The value of these crops began to fall as more families created farms and began to grow crops throughout the west, including Marceline. Because the train was the principal way of moving goods to markets in America's greatest cities, railroad executives began to raise fares, thus lowering the profit made by individual farmers. As a result, the agricultural community frequently breaks even every year, or loses money in some unlucky seasons owing to droughts or other environmental disasters.

When his farm suffered losses due to the poor value of apples countrywide in 1909, Elias devised a strategy to keep some produce until prices rose. He sold enough apples to pay off some obligations, but he kept the remainder of his crop. Elias enlisted the services of Herbert and Raymond to transport his supply of autumn's apple harvest from the family barn late in the season and into the orchard. The three men worked hours spreading straw between the rows of apple trees, then arranging the fruit into waist-high pyramids on top of the straw. They placed straw on top of the fruit after the heaps were finished, then covered the layers with earth, providing natural refrigeration and protection from the elements and pests.

As the winter continued, the price of fresh fruit fell. Elias would go to the orchard a few days a week, often in bitter cold and wind, to unearth his fruit, which had kept fresh due to the ground freezing on top of the piles.

While this idea was quite clever, Elias realised that it would not be able to supply the money his family required year after year. Taking a cue from Debs and the Populists, he chose to reach out to the larger agricultural community in Marceline in order to effect change for folks in the region. Initially, he attempted to enter state politics by campaigning as a socialist for a seat in the Missouri state legislature. Unfortunately, the Missouri state government, like the federal government, had little interest in smaller groups outside of the traditional two-party system.

Instead, Elias chose to address individuals in his immediate circle of influence: his fellow farmers in Marceline. Looking for a convenient spot to meet with his neighbours, he persuaded the Knights of Pythias, a fraternal organisation with a lodge above Zurcher's Jewellers on the corner of Kansas Avenue and Ritchie Avenue, to let him host a gathering for his other apple producers in the region. In order to demonstrate to his fellow struggling farmers how good life could be if not for the 'evil capitalists' who took advantage of them, he went to Ed Hayden's, a local grocer, and ordered several kilograms of oysters.

The tasty oysters impressed the farmers who attended Elias' meal. Many of them had only heard of the delicacy, but due to the difficulties of living in a farming village, they had never eaten anything of this calibre. As the lunch came to an end, Elias looked around the room and noticed many of his peers smiling. He reasoned that with their stomachs full, now was the greatest time to present his case.

Moving to the front of the meeting, the farmer used his abilities as a guest preacher at the family church in Chicago to suggest that the farmers unionise and collectivise their efforts as members of a Marceline chapter of the Society of Equity. This organisation, he continued, was a sort of farmer's union that would fight against the railroads and bankers' injustices. The Society would establish grain elevators and cold storage facilities in town so that all farmers could retain their extra crops until prices stabilised, just as he had done with his own bumper crop of apples the previous winter. This concept would also allow Marceline's farmers to wield negotiating power: if railroads made their rates too high, the farmers would simply store their harvests in community storehouses. When railroads couldn't make a profit due to a shortage of agricultural fares, they were compelled to decrease their prices, benefiting farmers the most.

Elias was dismayed to see the smiles on his audience's faces as he spoke. Many people's attention began to wander, and a few actually got up and departed their tables. Later that evening, when his audience had gone home, the man who wanted justice for other farmers reflected on what had gone wrong. He eventually realised the town existed as a result of the railroad. Yes, railroad costs were extortionate for Marceline farmers, but without the Santa Fe expansion, none of the farmers would have the land that had been in their families for generations. Many of Marceline's enterprises, such as the coal mines and newly created oil fields, directly serviced the railroad, making the farmers' connection with the Santa Fe Railroad both favourable and bad. Elias realised that if they banded together to unionise against the railroad, they would literally be severing the hand that was feeding them.

After his attempt to improve the family's financial situation by forming an alliance with his fellow farmers failed, Elias began to demand the rest of the family to shoulder more of the burden and contribute more. While he expected his four sons to work for free on the farm, he also requested that they do odd jobs around town to help balance the income lost due to the farm's difficulties.

Roy frequently travelled town to accomplish little things and brought his younger brother along to assist. On a bright afternoon, the two went to the local undertaker's and washed Mr Hutchenson's hearse. Unfortunately for Roy, he did the majority of the work: as he scrubbed the buggy clean, Walter reclined in the back, hands folded across his chest, pretending to be a corpse. When someone passed by or stopped to speak with Roy, the youngster swiftly sat up; although some were taken aback, others were familiar with young Walter and his antics and were unsurprised by his prank.

Roy was similarly inspired by his father's efforts on the family farm to start his own money-making endeavour. Roy planted rows of popcorn on his own after convincing Elias to give him an acre of land. He worked in the field all summer, ploughing, seeding, watering, weeding, and finally gathering the hard kernels. The young guy walked downtown to the train station and sold his produce to travellers wandering around the platform or waiting for the train while it was serviced, after putting them in small bags he had salvaged from confectionery.

Flora used her creative and culinary skills to help create extra money for the family in addition to completing her duties as a rural wife and mother. Flora kept her own vegetable garden to help with expenses. During seasons when she had an abundance of food, she would often sell it to neighbours and townspeople; she was especially well-known for her outstanding grated horseradish, which was used in coleslaw and other midwestern specialties.

Flora Disney was also well-known in town for the butter she made. Following the purchase of sweet cream from the Marceline Creamery Company, the hardworking woman would spend several days churning and painstakingly adding ingredients to ensure that her product was as creamy as possible, with the proper balance of sweet and salty. She would load up the family buggy and ride to the grocer's, where she would exchange the butter for goods and money to increase the family's income.

Flora Disney's sweet cream butter drew customers from the countryside and even from outside the city. Elias instantly recognized the worth of his wife's butter and forbade his children from indulging in it so that there would be more to market. Flora began to butter the backside of her children's bread before delivering it to them at meals to thwart her husband's expectations, pitying her children and tapping into her mischievous streak that had been handed down to her youngest son.

In order to gain more money, Elias rented an additional 40 acres of land from his brother Robert, offering to let Herbert, 19, and Raymond, 17, work a portion of the land for a little fee. After a hard season of work in 1907, the two industrious young men discovered that they had earned $175 from the sale of their produce. The guys saved the majority of the money, and decided to indulge themselves with a gold watch and chain from Zurcher's, a new jewellery store that had opened only a few years before.

The males proudly wore their watches and chains on their breasts the entire way home, but Elias was repulsed by their lavish expenditures. He made it obvious to his sons that purchasing the accessories was irresponsible given the circumstances.

"And what are you going to do with the remainder of your earnings?"" the older Disney inquired, half-jokingly.

"Well," Herb continued, his gaze fixed on his brother. "We would like to purchase a heifer and a colt to help make our tract of land more sustainable."

"Goshen Land!" Elias sighed heavily. He went on to explain that as members of the Disney family working on land he'd leased from Robert and sharing the family's resources, such as food and housing, their revenue was designed to help offset the farm's obligations. Herbert and Raymond's features gradually changed from subservient to stony and indignant as he spoke, but their father was too preoccupied preaching about the family's need to work together for survival to notice.

Herbert and Raymond grew increasingly frustrated with their father's conversation and his inability or unwillingness to see them as men who had earned their living through hard work, rather than as boys, over the course of the evening and the next day while working in the fields. Herbert unhitched the horse from the plough and rode into town that afternoon, withdrawing all the money from his and Raymond's bank accounts. Following a magnificent lunch served by Flora that evening, the two guys pretended to be exhausted and excused themselves to bed. When the house had quieted down, the brothers gathered their belongings, opened their bedroom window, and stepped out onto the porch.

While they may have felt a sense of sorrow for abandoning their mother and other siblings, their annoyance with Elias and his unyielding expectations overshadowed their grief, and the two raced into town and to the Santa Fe train station together. Using some of their farming earnings, they each bought a ticket for the 9.30pm train to Chicago, riding the night train north, away from Marceline, never to return to live at the Disney farm.

Elias considered his eldest sons' departure as a betrayal of the worst kind, but instead of venting his rage on the rest of the family, he poured himself even more into the farm, filling the void left by Herbert and Raymond's departures. Roy went to Park School, which is located west of downtown Marceline, and helped out with chores before and after school, as well as on weekends. Elias and Flora both agreed that, because their two youngest children were so close in age, and because extra help was required on the farm, they would keep Walter out of school until Ruth was old enough to enrol at Park School. As a result, he assisted with agricultural tasks for the next year, continuing to mill the sorghum and care for the livestock. Flora, not wanting her youngest son to lag behind, began teaching Walter to read in order to prepare him for the rigours of public school.

Walter and Ruth were scheduled to start at Park School in the fall of 1908. Over the next few years, Walter realised that schooling was not his strong suit: he preferred fantasising and sketching to learning, even painting on the pages of his McGuffey's Eclectic Reader and carving W.D. Not once, but twice, into his wooden desk. Miss

Brown, his teacher, found the youngster to be 'ornery,' refusing to participate in his assignments when she attempted to concentrate his attention.

While the academic side of school did not appeal to Walter, the artistic side did. Park School chose to stage its own version of Peter Pan after the success of Maude Adams' performance at Carter's Opera House. Walter auditioned and was cast as the protagonist in the play. Walter Disney intended to bring the story to life and involve his audience in the action from a young age. Desperate to fly like his role, he persuaded Roy to design a hoist and tackle apparatus that would allow him to soar above the crowd.

Walter met his first love and 'dream girl' during his stay at Park School: Mrs Eugenia Moorman, the young wife of Marceline's superintendent of education. Walter was not a bashful child, but he struggled to comprehend how to capture the attention of his object of adoration. Fortunately for him, when Elias and Flora went out of town for the evening, they asked Mrs Moorman to babysit Walter and Ruth. That evening, while mom was putting him to bed, he was even more shocked by his luck.

"Do you fear sleeping alone in the dark?"" The caring young lady inquired of the small youngster.

The youngster assured her that he was.

Mrs Moorman slipped into bed with the youngster, who didn't know much more than that people in love slept in the same bed, not wanting her charge to throw a scene and hoping his parents would let her babysit again.

One issue Walter hadn't considered was his bedwetting problem.

When he awoke many hours later in a panic, he discovered the opposite half of his bed unoccupied. It was never clear whether Mrs. Moorman had left the bed due to his incontinence or for another reason.

Love was frequently accompanied by loss. Erastus 'Grandpa' Taylor died on January 20, 1909. Not only did 7-year-old Walter lose the father he loved listening to and learning from, but the Disneys' adoptive family, the Taylor-Phillips-Cranes, also lost their patriarch. Every day, as he opened his front door, he felt the empty agony of loss as he saw Grandpa Taylor's modest house across the street, its clapboard siding, plate glass windows, and beautiful white screen door less charming without Grandpa Taylor hobbling around the yard or sitting in his chair. Elizabeth Taylor had moved out of the home she'd constructed with her husband following his death and into the home of her son Winfield, who lived nearby.

Walter was awakened in the middle of the night some months later by yelling outside his bedroom window. He opened his eyes groggily and spotted a flickering orange light on the wall near his bedroom door. Walter's brass bed creaked as the boy's older brother crawled out from beneath the covers and crept to the window. Roy exclaimed as he drew the curtains aside from the window. Walter jumped out of bed and dashed to his brother's side, crawling up into the dormer's window seat to gaze out. A furious fire had enveloped Grandpa Taylor's home across the street, with a horse-drawn fire engine and bucket brigade attempting to extinguish the flames. The boys spotted their father's tiny figure attempting to assist, but it soon became clear that their efforts were worthless as the roof collapsed inward and the grass surrounding sizzled.

"It's like the whole world is on fire," Walter remarked. While it is obvious that this was the observation of a small boy learning to process trauma in the context of his entire world, figuratively he wasn't far off: the idyllic life of the boy who had fully embraced the charm and simplicity of small-town community was about to be stolen from him in much the same way that his elderly friend and visual reminder of him had been.

While Elias had had some success on the farm during the family's years in Marceline, he lacked farming ability and was frequently looked down on by his colleagues due to his ineptitude. This, combined with his lack of aid as a result of Herb and Ray's departure, made it difficult for him to keep up with the work required for farming. A drought hit the area near the end of the decade, not only preventing rainwater from falling on the fields, but also causing the family well, from which Elias drew irrigation water, to dry up.

Illness began to spread across the Disney farm when some of his livestock became ill, and Elias's overwork led to him acquiring diphtheria. In his extremely debilitated state, necessitating hospitalisation at times, Elias was unable to finish the labour required to turn a profit on the farm, delegating numerous jobs to Flora, Roy, and Walter, none of whom possessed the knowledge required to make the family endeavour a success. The final straw was the eventual collapse of crop prices, a disaster Elias had battled so hard to avoid at his downtown oyster supper at the Knights of Pythias lodge only a few years before.

After much deliberation, Elias and Flora decided it was time to sell the farm and pursue new prospects abroad. Robert, who was living in Kansas City with his wife Margaret, seemed to be doing well in the city's economy and pushed his older brother to join him. Elias decided to auction off the animals and farming equipment in order to clear the family's assets in Marceline. Walter and Roy were assigned to go across the countryside and into town, putting up signs announcing the auction and the many goods for sale. A pre-auction sale was held for the Disneys' neighbours, and several of the draught animals were sold, breaking Walter's heart. The family abandoned the farm in 1910, relocating into a smaller home at 508 Kansas Avenue, much closer to downtown Marceline; rather than leaving immediately for Kansas City, the family elected to stay until the conclusion of the school year. Fortunately for Walter, his family's new home was right next door to the Moormans.

The sound of a high-pitched whining attracted Roy and Walter's attention one afternoon while parked along Kansas Avenue to sell hay from the farm. The boys looked across the street to see what was making the ruckus and discovered a young colt tethered to a hitching post. It had been born on the family farm and had started crying when it recognized the Disney brothers. Walter went across the street to embrace the pony's head, and Roy eventually had to grab his little brother off the animal and walk him away before things got out of hand.

The boys piled into the buggy for the ride home, their old horse

Charlie nibbling on a feed bag peacefully. Something frightened their horse as they drove north on Kansas Avenue toward home, and he bolted. Because the buggy was ancient, the handbrake no longer operated. Roy did everything he could to slow Charlie down, pulling on the reins and shouting directions, while Walter gripped the cart hard to avoid sliding off.

"We need to jump off before we crash, Walter!" Roy summoned his brother.

"No!" Walter cried back, his iron grasp on the cart's handrail tightening.

"Alright," Roy said. "Take this," he said, passing one of the reins to his brother while holding the other. The eldest brother's stomach fell as he realised they were approaching the crest of one of the town's major hills; if he couldn't get Charlie to stop, this wasn't going to end well. Roy pushed on the left rein, leading the horse towards a grove of woods, leaning to the left as much as he could without falling off the buggy. Charlie avoided the trees, but the cart did not, and it collided with them, pulling the horse to a halt. Residents from surrounding homes heard the ruckus and ran into their yards to assist the lads. Fortunately, neither youngster was hurt, and neither the cart nor the horse suffered significant damage.

With the choice to go to Kansas City made, the Disneys were not alone in their grief: the Taylor-Phillips-Crane family, who had adopted them as one of their own, felt the anguish of abandoning people they had grown to love over the previous five years. Manly Howe Taylor even agreed to take care of the farm after the family left until it could be sold in November 1911. Flora attended her last Rural Home Circle meeting on May 15, 1911, and was so upset over leaving her friends that she neglected to fulfil her club role of preparing to present current developments in her family's life. According to the club minutes, it was considered and unanimously agreed upon by the club's twenty-one members that a souvenir teaspoon would be delivered to Flora as a parting gift on her departure for Kansas City.

Elias, Flora, Roy, Walter, and Ruth said their goodbyes to the charming rural town they had grown to love and the people they had grown to love even more, loaded their belongings at the same train station along the Santa Fe Railroad that they had arrived on, and moved on to their next adventure. Both Elias and Walter looked out the window as their dreams drifted away behind them: the former, leaving behind his hope to establish himself as a small-town farmer raising his children with small-town morals, while his youngest son left behind the town that had brought him so much life. Little did the child know that his future home, Kansas City, Missouri, would play an even bigger role in shaping him into the man he would become.

Chapter Eight: The Paper Route

While agriculture dominated most of Missouri life, one thing in particular influenced nearly every Missourian during the second half of the nineteenth and early twentieth centuries: the railroad. Massive population growth occurred as railroads expanded throughout Missouri, both in small agricultural communities like Marceline and large metropolitan areas like St. Louis, and from small towns on the Mississippi like Hannibal to cities along the Missouri River like Kansas City. During the latter few decades of the 1800s, nearly every town created throughout the state was located along one of the major rail lines, offering service to locomotives and passengers similar to that given by the Santa Fe in Marceline.

The presence of the railroad in these communities frequently resulted in the arrival of important industries. For example, when Kansas City became a major hub for nearly a dozen different railroad lines in the 1870s, it quickly became a railhead for cattle drives, in which herders known as cowboys pushed thousands of head of cattle from the south to the railroad before slaughtering and shipping the animals to major cities in the east. Armour and Company, a meat packing company with a branch in Kansas City, grew as a result of the area's thriving cattle sector, increasing canned beef production from roughly 779,000 units in 1880 to more than 4 million units just five years later. The success of corporations like Armour resulted in improvements to Kansas City's own stockyards, which are located along the Missouri River in a neighbourhood known as the West Bottoms. Between the yards' creation in 1871 and 1901, the number of animals slaughtered in Kansas City tripled, with other new enterprises popping up to challenge Armour and Company's success.

Throughout the Midwest of the United States in the 1870s, a devastating plague of grasshoppers devastated millions of dollars' worth of crops. Farmers and their families were particularly drawn to the prospects that industry and transportation infrastructure afforded in Kansas City, preferring to settle on the riverbank metropolis rather than risk their fortunes in the fields. As a result of this rush of migration, Kansas metropolis's population expanded from around 132,000 to 164,000 during the last decade of the nineteenth century, making it the second largest metropolis west of the Mississippi River, trailing only San Francisco, California.

With this expansion came additional industry. By 1900, about forty rail lines crisscrossed the city, serving as the principal route of transportation for livestock, wheat, and other agricultural products. Elevators and grist mills were built to store and process grains, sawmills were built to chop lumber, and infrastructure was built to serve the hundreds of trains that came through town every week.

With trains rumbling down iron tracks, horse-drawn carriages sharing the streets with early autos, and the rare steamboat sloshing over the murky waters of the Missouri River, Kansas City was soon a bustling hub of industry, business, and transportation. Industry emitted smoke and steam into the atmosphere, while the surge of people moving to the city, both native-born Americans and immigrants, polluted the ground.

William Rockhill Nelson, the new owner and editor of The Kansas City Star, began pushing for city beautification and civic improvements as early as the 1880s. As the City Beautiful Movement swept the United States, asking for better city planning, architecture, parks, and pollution controls to improve the lives of middle-class urban people, this campaign gained traction. Nelson began planning for open spaces and enormous parks for his burgeoning metropolis with landscape architect George E. Kessler, with a new boulevard system championed by Kessler and costing around $40 million to be finished in 1910. Kansas City had nearly 2,000 acres of parks, 700 acres of parkways, and 90 miles of boulevards by 1920.

The bustling business hub attracted middle-class Americans who were impressed by the opportunity for investment, the beautiful green spaces, and the growing suburbs that began to spread out from the city's downtown, rather than low-skilled industrial labourers, immigrants, or failed farmers looking for new opportunities. More leisure activities, such as vaudeville halls, theatres showing moving pictures, and amusement parks, were lured to the area to entertain the area's middle-class populace.

As a result, when the train bringing the Disney family arrived at Union Depot in Kansas City's West Bottoms neighbourhood in June 1911, Walter's new home was as far from what he was used to as it could be. Stepping off the train, the three children noted a difference in the air: although the fresh breeze in Marceline typically smelled like sweet grass, the stagnant air of Kansas City's West Bottoms was sour, with the stink of murdered cattle not far away.

Uncle Robert had dispatched a buggy to transport the family and their belongings southeast to the opposite side of town, where they had rented a little cottage at 2706 East 31st Street. Flora despised the new place and was relieved that they were only renting for a short time. While she had become accustomed to having an outhouse in their Marceline farmhouse, using one in their Kansas City backyard provided much less privacy owing to the metropolitan environment of their new property. Flora was also irritated since the property was on a busy street, and as a result, the tram line frequently went by. She made her husband aware of her dissatisfaction with the lack of privacy, noting that tram passengers could look into the front parlour. Elias' response to his wife's objections was to hang curtains.

Shortly after moving in, Elias and Roy went downtown on July 1st to the red brick building that held The Kansas City Star, responding to an advertisement for the opportunity to purchase a paper route. Approximately 700 subscribers were served by Delivery Route No. 145, which ran along 27th Street in the north, 31st Street in the south, Prospect Avenue in the west, and Indiana Avenue in the east, a total of twenty-four residential blocks. While many of the subscribers received both The Morning Times and The Kansas City Evening Star, the route also had 176 Sunday edition subscribers.

The Star was initially hesitant to give Elias, 51, ownership of the paper route because they feared he was too elderly and, as a result, would be unable to perform the obligations of the job. They were, however, ready to sell the paper route to Roy, who was 17 at the time. Elias paid more than $2,100 for the route's rights and received a contract and map of the route in exchange.

Elias didn't have enough money to pay delivery boys or newsies to sell the papers after abandoning Marceline and losing his investment in the failing farm. He anticipated his two youngest boys to contribute to the family business instead. Every day, Roy and his 9-year-old son Walter would get out of bed at 3.30 a.m. to greet the horse-drawn cart that brought the newspaper to their house. The brothers would take a stack of papers and start distributing them along the route, which fortunately included the Disney home, which served as a base to pick up additional papers throughout the morning.

According to their father's instructions, Walter and Roy were precise in how they positioned the newspapers. Elias, who was already in his forties, had become dissatisfied and unhappy as a result of his multiple failures in his various occupations as a hotel owner, railroad machinist, construction worker, residential contractor, and farmer. To avoid the shame of failure as the de facto owner of the paper route, he made it a point to teach his kids how to correctly leave the Star for its paying customers.

Elias wanted to make sure that his customers saw the difference in service that his family delivered. While delivery guys frequently rolled newspapers and hurled them into yards from the back of a bicycle, Elias forbade his sons from doing so. Instead, he anticipated the personal service of hand-delivering the newspaper to each door so that customers would not have to leave their homes to receive their publications. Elias also expected his two delivery guys to protect their merchandise from the elements: whatever newspaper he wasted would have to be reimbursed later by the Star. Instead, he told Walter and Roy to lay a stone or a block on top of the folded paper on windy days and inside the customer's screen door on rainy days to keep it from getting wet. Everyone knew where the newspaper delivery guys resided because of the value placed on community and one's neighbours at the turn of the century. If little Walter did something wrong, such as forgetting to secure a paper or accidentally missing a house, his father was informed, and discipline was imposed. While Roy was irritated that his father was still physically disciplining him at the age of 18, he was much more irritated that his father expected him and his younger brother to work for free. The boys were paid a monthly allowance ($3 for Roy and 50 cents for Walter), but their hard work as newspaper delivery boys earned them accommodation and board.

Walter and Roy went home after finishing the course, where they ate breakfast prepared by Flora. The rest of their morning and afternoon were spent enjoying the many activities that the city had to offer. Roy would occasionally pay for Walter and Ruth to ride the tram to Electric Park, which is located along Brush Creek near the intersection of 46th Street and The Paseo. The Heim Brothers constructed Electric Park north of Kansas City in 1899 as a way to sell more beer produced by their brewery in the East Bottoms. When this park became popular, the brothers decided to relocate it to a larger plot of land south of the city. The amusement park was a huge hit with Kansas City residents, with visitors able to swim in a vast lake, ride a roller coaster, explore a fun house, and watch shows. After nightfall, more than 100,000 lights illuminated the grounds and its myriad attractions, giving the park a fresh lease on life. While the city government banned the brothers' second amusement park from selling liquor, the Disney children were exposed to several other forms of moral turpitude, such as dance halls and women's exposed flesh. While Elias had little control over Roy's enjoyment of Electric Park, he was angry to find that his two youngest children were running around there and prevented them from entering its gates. As a result, whenever Walter felt like taking in the sights and sounds of the park, he would ride the tram south and stand with his face between the fence's bars, observing the commotion within.

Roy also involved his siblings in activities closer to home. He often played horseshoes in the backyard with Walter and Ruth, or taught them how to play tennis, and on rainy days they played pinochle in the parlour. On rare occasions, the trio would go to a local theatre to watch a movie at Roy's cost or to the drugstore to buy a bag of candy.

Elias and Flora enrolled their children in school in the fall of 1911: Roy entered his senior year at Manual Training High School, while Walter and Ruth began second grade at Benton Grammar School. The boys' daily obligations on their father's newspaper route continued, and as the Star switched from cart and buggy to automobile delivery, the papers were dropped off at the Disney home at 2.30 a.m., necessitating the boys to get up even earlier. Walter and Roy would spend the next several hours delivering papers around the neighbourhood before stopping at home for a quick breakfast and dashing off to school.

Walter was not an ideal student at Benton Grammar, as he had been at Park School in Marceline. He spent a lot of time daydreaming or scribbling in the margins of his textbooks. The child was unable to concentrate, most likely owing to a lack of sleep, and instead spent hours developing his interest in creative expression. His tasks and paintings were frequently imaginative, much to his teacher's displeasure. In one case, when asked to draw a field of flowers, the imaginative boy chose to depict the flowers with human faces instead of buds and arms ending in hands instead of leaves.

With every day's discharge from school, Walter dashed home, where he met Roy to organise the evening version of the paper before making his way across the neighbourhood to deliver 635 individual copies of the Evening Star. After Flora kept the boys' food warm, the boys completed some homework, followed by some peaceful reading time when Walter relished a novel by Twain or Dickens, before going to bed early the next day to do it all over again. Unfortunately, he was so busy that he had no time to play or interact with the other kids in the neighbourhood. To make up for his lack of recreation, Walter would frequently find himself in the early morning hours playing with the toys that children along the paper route had left on their porches before proceeding on to the next house.

When 1911 turned into 1912, 10-year-old Walter's paper route grew even more challenging when a series of blizzards swept throughout the American Midwest, dropping more than 170 cm of snow on Kansas City. Even the prospect of an early spring was dashed, with more than 100 cm falling in March 1912. Elias, ever the diligent worker and aware of the significance of revenue to maintain his family, had high expectations for the paper route during this harsh winter. Walter and Roy continued to get up early, bundling up as best they could and making their way through knee-high accumulations, the night-time winds whipping by, making their eyes moist and their faces chapped. Walter would have to climb over snowdrifts higher than himself to get to a subscriber's front door, frequently tumbling through the thin layer of compacted snow down to his waist, snow crumbles making their way up his trouser legs and down into his shoes.

Fortunately for him, his route included a series of apartment complexes, where he could thaw out in the steam-heated lobbies and halls. Walter would frequently stop in the flats to sit close to a heater to warm himself before returning to the cold, inevitably nodding off before springing awake in a panic that he had slept through the rest of his route.

Flora decided to use her abilities as a homemaker to supplement the family's income, as the paper route was the family's primary source of revenue. Flora imported cream from the Marceline Creamery Company on a weekly basis, using her Marceline contacts. Flora would spend days making her famous butter after Elias picked up the cream from the Railway Exchange office in downtown Kansas City. Elias also requested fresh eggs from a Marceline farmer, which was a costly luxury for city inhabitants in the early 1900s.

Elias thought it would be strange for a grown man to deliver newspapers, so he always used his two sons as delivery boys. However, his pride and work ethic made him feel bad that he wasn't doing anything to support the family. Flora would load the cream and fresh eggs onto a cart and walk about the neighbourhood selling the farm-fresh food to his neighbours once the cream was turned into butter.

Elias would occasionally experience a flare-up from his previous diseases of malaria or diphtheria, rendering him unable to make the deliveries. Flora would instead take Walter out of school for the day because he was more familiar with the newspaper route than she was, and the two of them would push the cart through the streets selling farm products to customers who paid for their farm products subscription service. Walter adored and respected his 43-year-old mother and didn't want her to exert herself, so he offered to push the cart down the street while his mother delivered the supplies. Flora, on the other hand, insisted on pulling the cart herself, much to the disgust of the lad.

During the 1911-1912 school year, Roy and Walter began to drift apart as they pursued their studies in the big city, acquiring new hobbies and friendships with vast groups of students, chances that weren't accessible in the little rural village of Marceline. The prevalence of girls in Kansas City was particularly appealing to Roy. While he had a steady relationship with Fleta Rogers in Marceline, the abundance of city girls enabled Roy to become more social in the world of eligible bachelorhood. This meant that there were more young males to compete against. He spent his allowance and money acquired from odd jobs to buy elegant suits and ties to please the young ladies in his social circle. Walter, who looked up to his older brother, would frequently wear one of his brother's new ties to school to show off to his friends. He'd always spill his lunch, which was usually chilli and beans, on his tie. Walter would quickly put the tie back on before meeting Roy on the sidewalk to give the afternoon edition, taking care to hang it up exactly the way Roy had. Unfortunately for the eligible bachelor, he would put on the tie for his next date, only to discover too late that it was still splattered with chilli and beans. Needless to say, Walter's chats with his younger brother later that night were not particularly nice.

Roy graduated from Manual Training High School in the spring of 1912. The young man had grown to be as tall as his father and had the same thin build. While Elias was growing fragile as a result of his multiple illnesses and maladies, and had recently celebrated his fiftieth birthday, Roy was a muscular specimen. He was irritated that Elias refused to compensate him for his efforts on the paper route, despite the fact that he officially owned it. One evening, while the boys lay in bed next to each other, Roy raised himself up on his elbow and jolted his sleepy brother awake.

"Hey, kid," Roy grumbled. Walter sprang awake, his eyes flying open to see his brother towering over him. "I'm fleeing to work in the harvest fields." I need you to stay and finish the route. And stop putting up with your father's beatings."

Young Walter begged his brother and best friend not to abandon him halfway between the worlds of slumber and awake. He did everything he could to keep his eyes open, convinced that if he stayed awake, he would be able to prevent his brother from departing at the appointed hour. When his door opened and Elias called for his two kids to get up for the route, Walter noticed Roy was no longer in bed next to him; instead, a mannequin made of coiled up bedsheets and garments was fashioned to look like his slumbering brother. After sending Walter off on his own, Elias and Flora sat and spoke about their third son's departure. Flora sobbed, wiping her tears on the corner of her apron, as Elias violently paced the kitchen floor, cursing the name Roy Disney. It was determined that extra lads from the neighbourhood would be employed to assist Walter on the route, but the father's wrath was unknowingly directed at his youngest son, intending to shape him into the man he had been unable to become himself.

Chapter Nine: The Performing Butch

For the young Walter Disney, life without Roy was a new challenge. While Elias was the strict disciplinarian who believed that holding the highest expectations of his children would result in good, productive people, Roy was kind and compassionate; while Elias was frugal with his money to ensure that the family's needs were met, Roy instead frequently spent his money on his little brother and sister by purchasing treats or small gifts for them, or occasionally taking them to Electric Park or the movies. Walter quickly became sidetracked by his daily life, which included school, work, and new companions in the absence of his best buddy and hero.

Flora thought she'd had enough of their leased home and convinced Elias that the family needed to buy a more permanent home soon after Roy's departure. Recognizing the value of living near the paper route, the family relocated a half-kilometre east to 3028 Bellefontaine Avenue, a small two-story house with white wood slat siding and a huge porch covering the front of the house supported by strong wooden pillars.

Living in a quiet neighbourhood rather than on a busy street made it easier for Walter and Ruth to form friendships with the kids next door. Mr. and Mrs. Pfeiffer and their two children, Kitty and Walt, who were the same age as Walter Disney, resided a short distance away on 41st Avenue. The two boys became fast friends, and Walter began spending his free time at Walt Pfeiffer's house rather than his own. The Pfeiffers were everything Elias wasn't: carefree, musical, cheeky, and inventive. Other than their names, Walter Disney and Walt Pfeiffer immediately discovered they shared a love of performance and joking about. In the Pfeiffers' back yard, the two youngsters quickly developed vaudeville shows, caricaturing themselves as a pair of Dutchmen, complete with strong Dutch accents. These spontaneous comedic acts were frequently done in front of the Pfeiffer family, accompanied by Walt's sister Kitty's piano playing. Walter rapidly became an unofficial member of the Pfeiffer family, striving to fill the void left by Roy's departure with his new friend in the time he wasn't in school or delivering his father's papers at their house. Walter and Walt were also inseparable during illness; one winter, when Walt Pfeiffer was bedridden with mumps, his artistic best friend sat by his side, giving him drawing lessons.

Walter's penchant for performance found its way into the classroom to relieve boredom over the next few years, much to the joy of his classmates. The most famous routine was Walter's 'Fun in the Photograph Gallery': entirely silent, the young actor would place his classmates in a variety of absurd motions, then stand behind a prop camera to imitate photographing them. Instead of a photograph, the camera would spray the unsuspecting target with a stream of water. Walter, being the good sport that he was, would always complete his performance by drawing a caricature of his subject to take with them.

Walter's inclination to play the class clown garnered the attention of the Benton staff, which they occasionally exploited. On Abraham Lincoln's birthday one year, fifth-grader Walter dressed up as the Great Emancipator, donning Elias's long church coat, donning a handmade stovepipe hat, sticking crepe paper to his chin to create a bushy beard, and putting shoe polish on his face to create a moustache. As he walked into class that morning, he began giving 'The Gettysburg Address' in the figure of Abraham Lincoln, dazzling his classmates but irritating his teacher. When Benton principal

James Cottingham found out, he planned to humiliate the youngster by giving him the largest possible audience to perform in front of: the entire school. Cottingham marched Walter from classroom to classroom to deliver the speech, but his ultimate purpose of punishing the boy was thwarted: Walter loved the limelight, and all of the students adored him.

Not all of Walter's professors were critical of him. In seventh grade, the youngster had the privilege of sitting in Miss Daisy Beck's classroom. Beck, who delivered papers before school, was sympathetic to the boy's situation: the warmth of the classroom as the day progressed often put the delivery guy, who had been awake since 2.00 a.m., to sleep. The kind teacher often let him sleep, knowing that if he was awake and fatigued, he wouldn't get much done. She also spotted the boy's creative ability and lured him by telling him that if he finished his classwork, he could spend the rest of the class time drawing. This inspired Walter, who finished his arithmetic quickly so he could doodle instead. Miss Beck was also Walter's track coach while he was at Benton, and he won a medal in the 80-pound relay event under her instruction.

Roy came to Kansas City in 1913, after a brief period working on Uncle Will Disney's farm near Ellis, Kansas, and then as a news butcher selling refreshments on the railroad. He lived in his own apartment and found work at the First National Bank of Kansas City. It was at this point that the young man met another teller, Mitch Francis. Francis informed Roy about a dance at a nearby social club one day, suggesting that they join Francis's two younger sisters to the dance. Roy wasn't a terrific dancer, but he agreed to avoid disappointing his new acquaintance. Later that evening, Roy arrived at the club with a suit and tie, taking care not to be covered in chilli or beans. When Francis and his two sisters arrived, the dance began: Roy was matched with Edna Francis, and the two had a fantastic evening. Following the success of the dance, Roy and Edna began spending more time together, and it was soon clear that the two would marry.

Walter was overjoyed that his big brother had returned to Kansas City and did everything he could to spend time with Roy. Roy, the boy's childhood playmate, was no longer a child: he had a career and a girl. When the elder Disney took Edna out, Walter's innocence didn't stop him from searching the neighbourhood for Roy. The pair frequently visited a nearby pharmacy soda fountain. Walter entered the institution after making his rounds to find his brother on his date. The pre-teen boy marched up to his older brother and requested for a cent to buy sketching paper. Roy, embarrassed and trying to hide his irritation, withdrew some cash from his pocket to appease the youngster.

It was soon clear that Roy was now living in a different world than Walter. Instead, Walter and Walt Pfeiffer started honing their vaudevillian performances by seeing shows at surrounding theatres for inspiration. Walter had taken on extra tasks to augment his paper route money, such as selling newspapers on a neighbouring corner, sweeping out a candy shop, and carrying medicine for a local druggist, all to help pay for his ticket to the plays. The two lads realised they could perform the same types of comic performances they saw on stage, and because of their young, they could generate a distinct attraction. They decided to enter a variety competition to put their hypothesis to the test. This would have to be done in secret, however, because Elias believed that vaudeville was coarse, immoral, and ruined one's character, and hence barred his younger children from attending such events.

On the night of the competition, Walter, pretending to be ill and going to bed early, crept out of his window and found Pfeiffer on the street outside his house, and the two boys walked to the local vaudeville hall together. Roy had somehow learned that Walter would be playing that evening and recommended to Elias and Flora that they spend an adult evening at the Agnes Theater while keeping their youngest son's performance a secret.

As Elias walked inside the vaudeville theatre, he was angry and ashamed that he was accompanied by Flora and Ruth, who was too young to spend the evening alone at home. The scent of smoke and booze lingered in the air, along with the noisy laughing and obscene jokes of inebriated men. Roy brought the family in and helped them choose a seat with a nice view of the stage.

The family sat through a number of acts, with Elias becoming increasingly angry as the evening proceeded, uneasy with the unpleasant comedy onstage and the audience's behaviour. The next act, 'The Two Bad Walts,' was introduced on stage as Elias was gathering his family to leave. Elias stopped dead in his tracks, his gaze fixed on the stage. He watched his youngest kid on stage dressed as Charlie Chaplin, wearing big shoes, his father's long church coat, a shoe polish moustache, and wielding a cane as the curtain parted. Elias fell into his seat, not wanting to draw attention to himself by rushing out of the hall, to witness his son's performance in grim chagrin as Walter and Pfeiffer chased each other across the stage in the slapstick way typical of Chaplin films. However, as the act progressed, Elias found himself with a grin on his face: not only were some of the jokes intelligent, but they were also humorous.

When the act was done, Elias signalled to the family to stand up and go. Walter, unaware that his parents and siblings had witnessed his performance, sneaked back home at the end of the evening 25 cents richer: he and Pfeiffer had earned fourth place and a cash prize.

After the first shock of his son's secret' had gone off, Elias preferred not to say anything about it. Perhaps there's something to this boy's passion for art and performance, Elias reasoned. As a result, when Walter asked to take some classes at the Fine Arts Institute of Kansas City at a nearby Y.W.C.A., learning technique in sculpting, sketching, and drawing animals and the human figure from local professionals, Elias relented because he believed it was important to hone skills in a specific hobby. However, he meant for his son to learn these abilities as a hobby only: art, he believed, could never be a viable vocation, as he'd learned from his failure as a fiddler in Denver.

As the twentieth century progressed, Kansas City began to modernise its technology and infrastructure. Elias decided in 1915 that the home on Bellefontaine needed to be enlarged to meet the needs of the family. Enlisting Walter's assistance, Elias used abilities he hadn't used since semi-professionally building houses with Flora in Chicago. Father and son worked together to create an addition to the back of the house, including an inner bathroom and space that could be used as a bedroom. Their success in constructing the expansion together led Elias to build a garage in 1916 to enable automobile access to the alley that ran behind the house, with Walter's assistance once again. However, Elias' temper flashed frequently when he felt agitated, either with his work or with his kid, resulting in the child evading tools thrown at him by his enraged father.

Even as a young teenager, this type of discipline was not an isolated episode for the lad. Elias would send his son into the basement to await a lashing if Walter made a mistake on the paper route or got into his typical mischief. Walter grew to despise the beatings, which had become increasingly frequent in the days after Roy's departure. Walter vowed to finally stand up to his father after remembering his brother's remarks to him the night he departed. When Elias lifted his hand to beat his son one afternoon, Walter caught the man's wrists and held them above their heads, preventing the discipline.

Elias engaged in a brief, half-hearted struggle with his youngest kid before allowing the power in his arms to wane. Realising he'd dodged corporal punishment, Walter cautiously let go of his father's wrists and took a step back, remaining on guard in case Elias's rage flared up again. Instead, the man's face slumped, and he softly turned and walked back up the steps, closing the door behind him. It was at that moment that the dad realised he no longer had control over his youngest son, and Walter never experienced another beating as punishment from his stern father again.

Elias quickly realised that with Walter standing up to him, the youngster was more likely to follow in his brothers' footsteps and leave in the middle of the night, leaving him with only the few lads he'd hired to deliver the papers and none of his children to assist. As a result, he decided to invest in his son and make things simpler for him in order to encourage him to keep working the route and staying with the family. When Walter persuaded his father to let him use his funds from side jobs to buy leather boots (which were both fashionable and functional), Elias surprised him with a pair for Christmas.

Walter was happy with his new boots since they not only kept his feet warm and dry during the winter deliveries, but they also gave him some credibility with the other lads in the neighbourhood, many of whom bullied the Marceline rural boy. Walter kicked a chunk of ice as he went down the side of the road one freezing evening after finishing his daily route. The chunk of ice, unbeknownst to him, included a huge nail, which punctured the toe of his new boot and was driven into his foot. Bending over, Walter grabbed the ice block and yanked on it, seeking to extract it from his boot. When it wouldn't budge, he tried removing the shoe, but this simply pushed the nail deeper into his foot, creating excruciating pain. Sitting on a curb, he began to scream out to everyone strolling by or riding the trams for assistance, but everyone dismissed him as a troublemaker. When people around saw that he was still yelling after many minutes, they came to aid. A buggy driver summoned a doctor, who indicated that he had nothing Walter could take for the discomfort. Instead, he solicited the assistance of a few men who held the boy's legs down while he extracted the nail from Walter's foot. His foot had swollen so much by this point that the only way to pull it out of the boot to assess the injury was to cut his prized new boot off.

Walter spent the next two weeks in bed recovering from his injuries. During this period, Elias relied on the assistance of his other delivery boys: the only time Walter got off the paper route was when he was delivering papers for his father. Instead, the budding artist drew from his bed, showing off his sketches to his mother and sister, who both complemented his work. To polish his artistic talents, Walter began to reproduce political cartoons from the Star and Times, much as he had done with Elias' copies of Appeal to Reason in Marceline. The child was able to examine the cartoons during his long hours in bed, with his drawing paper by his side and a newspaper strewn across his lap. He was particularly interested in cartoonists' depictions of humans and animals, symbolism, and wit. Walter's love of art and drawing evolved into a desire to turn his hobby into a vocation at this point. He'd made his decision: he'd become a newspaper cartoonist.

Walter soon found himself in a transitional era from infancy to young adulthood as the second decade of the twentieth century advanced, becoming increasingly conscious of the greater world around him and his place in it. The world erupted in late summer 1914, when the First World War engulfed Europe. While young men in France and Germany quickly recruited and marched off to war, the United States continued its isolationist policy: the German Kaiser and his army had little effect on America. As thousands of European immigrants began to select sides, tensions in cities across North America began to grow. As a result, the general people followed suit, embracing Britain and its allies while retaining the basic policy of isolation and refusing to move troops or supplies across the Atlantic. The United States government began generating wartime propaganda to persuade its citizens to assist its allies, and political cartoonists for major newspapers began to create articles reflecting on the war, the enemy, and events taking place overseas. It was into this context that Walter Disney, who had intended to become a political cartoonist himself, was thrown, causing the young man to become even more conscious of the world and its goings-on outside Missouri.

Walter began to perceive himself as a member of the collective, rather than an isolated individual who was not a part of the larger community, as a result of his growing global perspective. On January 27, 1917, Walter made his way to the Kansas City Convention Hall, where he and every other newsboy employed by The Kansas City Star had been invited to a showing of the silent picture Snow White. As he sat in his chair, he was one of hundreds of boys and young men who risked the elements to bring news and commentary to Kansas City residents' front doors.

However, the screening of Snow White had a greater influence on Walter than simply praising the paperboy for his efforts. The boy sat riveted in the dim light of the room, oblivious to the swarm of kids surrounding him shouting, throwing objects, and climbing over chairs: his focus was fixed on the action on the screen in front of him. Marguerite Clark, the film's star, caressed wild critters in her small hands and chatted to them. He chuckled as he watched the seven dwarfs hard at work in their mine, sobbed with them as they lamented the princess asleep on her bike, and cheered for pleasure when the prince kissed her awake. It was one of the most ambitious entertainment presentations Walter Disney had ever seen, and the elaborate sets, colourful characters, rich detail, and engaging plot would shape how he created entertainment for the rest of his career.

Everything changed for Walter in June 1917, when Elias discovered a new financial possibility. Elias had been investing in a Chicago jelly and soda plant called O-Zell since 1912, hoping that he might earn a profit and become wealthier than relying exclusively on the paper route. Much to Walter's annoyance and anger, Elias was even making his son invest the money he'd gained selling the Star on street corners, in an attempt to educate him how to be wise with his money rather than simply hoarding or wasting it. Elias was especially interested in O-Zell's moral benefits since its owner, Ernest A. Scrogin, decided to make fruit soda as an alternative to the alcoholic beverages that had become popular in Chicago. Thus, Elias paid Scrogin $1 a share for 2,100 shares of O-Zell stock, investing not just in the company but also in a moral and dry America.

Over the next two years, Scrogin continued to write to Elias, asking for more money, confident that one of his most prominent investors would continue to back the company as it perfected the formula for its Oriental Fruit Beverage. Between 1912 and 1918, the Disneys bought over 7,000 more shares, but O-Zell never put anything on the market for public consumption.

With the public market not showing much interest in the available drinks, O-Zell decided to produce a line of jellies, jams, and preserves, which appeared to be more appealing to the typical consumer. Scrogin realised he was in over his head with this new discovery and needed all hands on deck. On March 6, 1917, Elias received a letter from O-Zell's CEO indicating that the investor needed to decide whether he was all-in on the company's success. Scrogin said that if he was, it would be in both Elias' and O-Zell's best interests if he moved to Chicago to help run the firm. Elias sent $16,000 to Scrogin to purchase an interest in the company and was appointed head of plant building as a result of the company's development into jams and jellies manufacture.

Flora opted to stay in Kansas City so Walter and Ruth could finish the school year, while Elias moved ahead to find a home for the family in Chicago, maintaining the same attitude she'd had in Marceline. Flora and Ruth packed their possessions and travelled by train from Kansas City to Chicago to join Elias, who had purchased a house at 1523 Ogden Avenue in west Chicago, when the children's studies ended in June 1917. It was determined that Walter would stay in Kansas City to enable the new owner of the paper route, who had inherited a far larger route than Elias had initially purchased in 1912 due to the Disneys' success in collecting new subscriptions, have a smooth transition. Walter was not alone in Kansas City: he stayed in the Bellefontaine house with his brother Herbert, his wife Louise, and their child Dorothy. Herbert had lately moved back in with his parents after pleading for Elias' forgiveness.

With the school year completed and the paper route successfully changing hands, 15-year-old Walter was looking for a summer job before returning to Chicago with his parents and sister for the autumn semester at his new school. Roy, who had previously worked as a news butcher, selling newspapers and refreshments to train passengers and on platform during pauses, proposed that his brother do the same. Walter, who had grown up in Marceline with a profound passion for trains, was delighted at the chance, and Roy borrowed him $30 to buy his initial stock of goods to sell.

Walter was engaged by the Van Noyes Interstate News Company and sent to operate on the Missouri Pacific route between Kansas City, Missouri and Denver, Colorado, a distance of around 1,000 kilometres. During his journeys, Walter would walk up and down the passenger car aisles, handing out snacks, beverages, chocolates, and cigars to the passengers. On his first day, the child opted to keep his supply stash, as well as empty bottles he could return for a deposit refund, in a freight car at the end of the train. While business was steady, the news butcher was concerned to see soldiers on his line throwing empty bottles out the window of the rushing train: it was the equivalent of throwing his money out the window. When the train came to a stop around lunchtime to replenish its supplies of water, sand, and coal, Walter went out onto the platform to try to sell to those socialising outside. When the whistle blew, Walter returned to the train, making his way to the back of the train to store his empty bottles and reload his supplies before returning up the aisle. However, he discovered that the freight car containing his supplies and empty bottles was no longer attached to the train: it had been detached and had been abandoned at the last station, along with his investment and revenue. On future journeys, Walter discovered that he didn't sell fresh fruit quickly enough; the majority of the fruit quickly deteriorated and attracted flies, resulting in the loss of much of the money he and Roy had put in the product.

Walter, having been instilled with hard effort and a reluctance to give up by his father, saw his misfortune as a learning opportunity and devoted himself to his job in order to deliver the finest service possible to his customers. Van Noyes' routes were so successful and pleasant that he added the Kansas City Southern and Missouri, Kansas & Texas Railroad lines to his repertoire. Walter also saw that he could sell to individuals who worked for the train as well as passengers. When the passenger cars weren't as packed, Walter would make his way up to the locomotive and sell chewing tobacco and cigars to the engineers and firefighters, who would let him ride on the engine till the next stop. Walter was in ecstasy, remembering his time on Uncle Mike's lap in Marceline and getting to observe the effort of driving a train firsthand.

Working for the Van Noyes Interstate gave Walter the opportunity to see the world outside of his hometown, which was particularly special for a youngster whose family had not been rich enough to travel outside of Marceline and Kansas City. Unfortunately, his innocence frequently got him into problems or put him in awkward positions. During a voyage between Kansas City and Downs, Kansas, the train halted overnight one evening. Walter checked into a motel and changed out of his Van Noyes outfit before venturing into town to investigate. A local cop noticed the unknown teenager peering into the windows of numerous businesses and suspected him of scouting the area for prospective crimes. When Walter stated that he was staying in town as an employee of the Van Noyes Interstate News Company, the officer refused to accept him and hauled him back to the train yards before the people there vouched for him.

On another occasion, Walter disembarked a train at Pueblo, Colorado for the evening before continuing on to his goal the next day. Because the young man was unfamiliar with the town, he inquired about lodging and was referred to a 'boarding home' within a large Victorian-era storefront. Walter felt decidedly upper-class as he stood on the sidewalk looking up at the building, which featured a big staircase going up to a hefty oak door, and windows enclosed by red velvet curtains edged with gold fringe.

When no one answered his knock, the fatigued young man pushed open the door to reveal a foyer equipped with plush couches, gilded furnishings, and a brilliant crystal chandelier. Beautiful young women a few years his senior sat in couples or small groups, talking quietly and occasionally casting sly glances at Walter. When she noticed the hesitant young man standing in the doorway, a full-figured woman entered the foyer, her eyes sparkling. Her painted face was adorned with a wide smile and a flurry of wild, red hair. She drew her bathrobe collar tighter around her neck and gave the young man a cool beer while he made his selection.'

Walter thanked the woman for her generous offer, his mind scrambling to figure out what kind of boarding establishment would serve alcoholic beverages to its guests. His attention was drawn to movement in his peripheral vision, and he looked up to see a young woman, the skin of her neck and upper chest red, guiding a cowboy down the steps. Walter stepped to the side to make room for the couple, watching as the young woman opened the door for the man, who grinned back at her over his shoulder as he went into the night and she closed the door behind him. Suddenly, he realised: this was no boarding house, but a bordello, and the 'choice' the matron had mentioned was which female would accompany him upstairs! He carefully opened the door and made his way down the front steps, nodding at a couple of the females seated close, before being propositioned again. At the conclusion of the summer, Walter counted up the money he'd made from his sales for the Van Noy Interstate News Company and realised he'd made almost nothing, instead forfeiting the $30 bond Roy had borrowed him to begin. However, his tenure on the trains provided him with a variety of experiences and reinforced many of Elias's ideals and morals, such as hard work, the need of treating others properly, and the resolve to give up. It also demonstrated that the young man did not want to settle for odd jobs or the 'next best thing' like his father, but rather wanted to establish a career that would last the test of time.

PART V: A LIFETIME OF EXPERIENCE – CHICAGO, ILLINOIS AND FRANCE, 1917–1919

Chapter Ten: Odd Jobs

Walter's stint as a news butcher on the Missouri Pacific came to an end as the summer of 1917 drew to a conclusion. He packed his belongings and left Herbert and his family at the Bellefontaine residence, returning to Chicago to Elias, Flora, and Ruth on Ogden Avenue.

Walter had enrolled as a student at McKinley High School for the upcoming autumn term. The 16-year-old immediately established himself as a regular contributor as an artist to the school newspaper, The McKinley Voice. Many of his cartoons included comments on current events, such as propaganda messages about the war raging over the Atlantic. One cartoon apparently asked young guys in the school if they would spend their summer vacation working or fighting as members of the United States military services. His drawings also served a personal purpose: shortly before Walter returned to Chicago, his brother Roy and Edna Francis's younger brother Mitch experienced a surge of patriotism and enlisted in the United States Navy. On 22 June 1917, Roy and Mitch were sworn in together and promptly dispatched to the Great Lakes Naval Station, about 60 kilometres from the Disney house in Chicago. Another of Walter's older brothers, Raymond Disney, had also enrolled, although in the Army rather than the Navy. Walter created propagandistic political drawings for The McKinley Voice to support his brothers who were serving overseas, as well as to contribute to the war effort because he was too young to enlist.

Walter spent his time outside of McKinley High School doing hobbies and working. He had no plans to become an illustrator at the time, but he knew he enjoyed drawing. To attend night school for illustration, the young creative persuaded his stern father that it was only a hobby, not a possible job. Walter was allowed to attend night sessions at the Chicago Academy of Fine Arts, where he studied under Chicago Tribune cartoonist Carey Orr. Orr, who satirised everyday news items and current events in his strip The Tiny Trib, was an idol to the aspiring artist. Orr's ecstatic pupil would eventually launch a similar column in his school newspaper, The Tiny Voice. Unfortunately, Walter discovered that the classes and styles taught at the Academy did not always match his abilities: while many of the courses taught the intricacies of producing still lifes and realistic drawings of people, the aspiring cartoonist discovered that his true passion was for humorous caricature. Walter had stopped attending night classes at the art school by early 1918, and had instead devoted himself to his work on The McKinley Voice.

For the young Walter Disney, art and drawing swiftly became all-consuming. His education began to suffer as he spent valuable class time drawing instead of studying. Instead of socialising like a 'normal' adolescent, Walter would attend school social events for artistic inspiration: seated on a chair along the wall, he would observe the other kids mingle and sketch their gestures, or he would occasionally draw trick images to amaze his friends and acquaintances.

Disappointed that he was too young to enlist like his siblings, the young patriot chose to help his community and country by working. Shortly after returning to Chicago, he reluctantly accepted odd jobs at O-Zell. He spent time washing out jelly jars, mashing up apples to generate the gelatinous pectin that made jellies thick, sealing the jars after they were full, and nailing together boxes for shipment while working in the jelly production facility. On one occasion, he was even requested to fill in as night watchman while the regular security guard was absent due to illness. Walter was extra alert because he knew the factory was in a high-crime neighbourhood and not far from the railroad tracks, where immoral or dangerous vagrants could stroll. When the plant manager handed him a.38 calibre handgun to serve as protection and enforcement upon his arrival for duty, it didn't assist his paranoia. That evening, while on his rounds, Walter kept all the lights on in the factory, convincing himself that doing so would make any potential thieves think twice when they saw the revolver the slim, young nightwatchman was carrying.

Walter was fortunate to reside in a city with an abundance of trains, which fueled his interest even more. Fortunately for him, he was able to find supplemental work at the elevated train line station on Wilson Avenue on days when work at O-Zell was scarce. He would leave school, go to the station, put on a cap and badge identifying him as a railway employee, and assist in loading and unloading people from the elevated train. Walter worked with his colleagues gatemen to manually open and close the train doors. Starting at the back of the train, the first gateman would ring his bell, indicating that all passengers had boarded and his doors were closed. This would cause the following gatemen to ring their bells, coach by carriage, until the sound of the bells reached the front of the train, alerting the conductor and engineer that the train was ready to leave the station. On one occasion, Walter, who was standing in the middle of the train platform, gave the signal too soon; fortunately, his error did not disrupt the remainder of the process and cause the train to depart before all passengers were secure.

However, neither of these occupations nor education seemed to please Walter. The war fever that swept the United States in the summer of 1917 weighed heavily on his conscience. On 6 April 1917, America officially became an aggressor in the First World War, following the resumption of Germany's unrestricted submarine warfare on 'neutral' American merchant vessels, a reversal of a German promise not to fire on those not considered belligerents. The United States and its citizenry engaged the domestic war machine, pumping out propaganda: even Walt Disney drew propaganda cartoons for McKinley's school newspaper's Tiny Voice section.

Chicago, as one of America's largest cities, became a major centre of patriotism and war fervour. During the summer and early autumn of 1917, the streets of the city seemed to be perpetually filled with war parades consisting of great columns of soldiers from the Great Lakes Naval Station, brass bands, contingents of American Red Cross workers, and floats covered in beautiful girls catcalling the young men passing by.

While Walter was staring up at the beauties perched atop a patriotic float one afternoon, one of them cried out to the throng, "Why don't you join up?" What's the deal with you? Are you a slacker or what?

Enlist! I challenge you!" The young man shook as goose bumps appeared all over his body. The females were conversing with him. Why didn't he come along? Roy and his older brother Raymond had also enlisted and were fighting for liberty. Wasn't it also his responsibility to serve democracy?

The problem was that he was only 16 years old, too young to join any branch of the US military.

The Disneys learned one early autumn afternoon that Roy was transferring to Chicago's Great Lakes Naval Station and would be passing through the city on his route north. It was unusual to hear from Walter's older brother: Elias had been so enraged by his son's betrayal in Kansas City, as well as his son's decision to enlist in the military, that he had tossed every unopened letter from Roy into the stove.

When it came time to meet Roy, Walter walked to the train station by himself to greet his brother. One of the first things he noticed was how well-dressed and mature his brother was in his Navy uniform. The two just had a few minutes to talk while sitting on a bench along the train platform. Other soldiers lingered about, interacting with one another or conversing with their own friends and family. When it was time for the troops to go, an officer yelled to them, "Fall in!" The two brothers stood up and hugged each other, exchanging well wishes. Roy gathered his belongings and began walking toward the column of men. When the officer noticed Walter standing beside the bench, watching his brother go away, he assumed he was one of the enlisted guys and marched over to him. "Come on, come on!" Did you not hear me? "Jump in!" Walter apologised, stating that he was not a military and had come to see his brother. The officer nodded, swung on his heel, and returned to his waiting troops.

As Walter Disney walked out of the train station that afternoon, back into the sun of an early October day in Chicago, he realised something: despite the fact that he had been working many jobs and preparing for an autumn term at McKinley High, none of them were gratifying. If he truly believed in what America stood for, he should enlist and be a part of the big conflict taking place in Europe.

Chapter Eleven: The Postman

As the war fever in America spread across the country in support of the blazing struggle in Europe, young Walter Disney got the bug. Propaganda argued that young men needed to enlist in order to stop the German Kaiser and the culture he was attempting to spread across the Atlantic, and that it was their patriotic responsibility to do so. Unfortunately, the minimum enlistment age was 17, and Walter was one year too young.

The school year started at McKinley High, but the young man's focus was elsewhere. Walter's desire to serve his country grew, but after becoming dissatisfied with the age restriction, he looked for alternative methods to aid. During this period, he devoted his heart and everything into The McKinley Voice, drawing his own propaganda cartoons for his column, The Tiny Voice. As inspiration, the aspiring artist kept a list of visual jokes termed a 'gag file' from which he would extract visual gags to place into his cartoons; many of these visual gags were inspired by the scores of vaudeville acts and silent films he had seen during his spare afternoons in downtown Chicago. To see if his jokes would elicit chuckles in his column, Walter realised he needed to test them on someone who lacked a sense of humour: his father. Walter would quietly bring up a hypothetical circumstance or tell his father a joke in passing during these gag tests with Elias, mindful of his hatred for his son's passion for art. True to his character, Elias would nod at his son and offer a nondescript compliment: "That's nice, Walter." On rare occasions, a few days later, the strict and serious patriarch would approach his youngest son while maintaining a serious demeanour. "I've been thinking about that joke you told me the other day," he'd say. "It's amusing, Walter. Very amusing." This reaction alerted him that, while the gag would not be able to break through his father's austere exterior, it would likely lead his classmates to chuckle in response. Even putting a comic perspective on the battle abroad didn't satisfy the convictions that drove him to join up.

As the school year drew to an end, Walter resumed his odd jobs at O-Zell and got a job as a postal carrier, following in his father's footsteps once more. Walter had a variety of jobs to complete on any given day while working at the Chicago Post Office. He worked as a sub carrier, picking up and delivering mail when the regular postmen were absent due to illness. He and his coworkers would take three or four different routes across downtown Chicago on any given day. Walter was able to use a horse and buggy on several instances, making it easier for him to gather enormous numbers of envelopes and packages. Senior postmen had taught one horse to walk the route and stop at specific points. Walter was told not to touch the reins and to let the horse pull him along the path. It took some time for him to figure out how the horse worked: after placing several letters and packages into the rear of the buggy, the horse would begin its trek to the next stop, leaving the irritated Walter waiting on the curb. Walter had to try to hurl himself into the moving cart or follow until the next pickup place when he knew the horse would stop because it had been trained not to respond to vocal directions. Unfortunately, the same charade would begin again after piling additional mail into the back of the buggy. It didn't take long for him to realise that the sound of the buggy door slamming was the horse's signal to begin moving towards the next halt; from then on, he quietly closed the door before climbing inside the cart.

Walter emerged from the lobby of a building, his arms full with envelopes, on one particularly stressful day when collecting mail from the hotels along Chicago's Grand Avenue, to find that the horse and buggy were no longer parked on the curb where he had left them. Running onto the street, he glanced up and down the street, but the large number of horses, buggies, trams, and motorcars made it difficult to locate the mail vehicle. Remembering that the horse had memorised the path, the terrified mail carrier began to hurry down the sidewalk, taking care not to drop any of the letters he was carrying. He took a side street, then another parallel to Grand Avenue, where he found the horse waiting for him on the other side of the hotel building; evidently, it had been trained to go around the block and wait for the postal carrier on the other side of the lobby, saving valuable time along the postal route.

Walter's journey also took him to the Grand Avenue Pier (today's Navy Pier), where tourists could board a steamer across Lake Michigan, as well as a port for freight being imported and exported from the lakeside city to other parts of the country. The 1,000-metre Grand Avenue Pier was a new addition to the city; originally opened a few years before in 1916, it also served as an outdoor recreation space as well as a jail for those who had evaded the American draft when the United States entered the First World War.

Walter rode a tram back to the post office with his mailbag on his back one day after collecting postcards from the mailboxes along the pier. It was a gorgeous day, and he enjoyed seeing people rush along the sidewalks, the diversity of hectic traffic on the streets, and the new towers being built, which are claimed as some of the world's tallest. He decided that since he had nothing else to do on this Sunday afternoon, he would pick up an extra route collecting letters around the city. When he returned to the post office, he hung his bag of postcards on a peg in the horse barn and brought out the buggy, which was already attached to his favourite horse, to complete the journey.

A few weeks later, Walter was sitting in the mailroom sorting mail for delivery, cracking jokes with his coworkers. He became aware that everything had gotten unusually quiet, and that his companions were no longer laughing. When he looked up from his stack of letters, he noticed that everyone's features had gone grave, almost a mix of surprise and terror - and they were all staring at him.

"Disney!" a voice from behind him said. Walter began. When he turned back, two tough-looking postal inspectors stood behind him.

"That's me," the young man mumbled.

"Come along with us," they said. As he was carried away, Walter stood up from his chair and cast a sidelong glance at his friends. His mind raced as he headed toward a nearby office, attempting to figure out what he had done wrong. What had happened to the delivery horse? Had he delivered mail to the wrong address by mistake? Whatever it was, it had to be bad because these guys seemed serious.

After entering an office, one of the inspectors shut the door; both sat on the opposite side of a table in the room from the young man, who was now trying to maintain his cool but secretly terrified.

"Did you get a bag of mail from the Grand Avenue Pier a few weeks ago?"", one inspector inquired.

"Yes, that's correct," the young postman replied. "How did you use it?". "I put it through the mail chute," Walter explained. "No, you didn't," the second officer said, pounding his fist on the table. "How did you use it?" Now, youngster, come clean!"

Walter leaped. His increasing dread made it more difficult to conceal his terror. A tornado of ideas raced through his mind. He remembers delivering the mail. What would his father think about this? Perhaps he didn't put the mail through the chute. What about Roy? What would he say? He didn't have to be concerned about his younger brother being imprisoned for mail fraud. When he looked down at his feet, they started moving in a circular manner, but it wasn't because he was moving them; the room had started spinning.

"Well, we'll tell you what you did with the bag of postcards, Disney," said the first postal inspector, who appeared to be speaking from a distance. "You hung it on a peg in the horse stable, and it's been hanging there for two weeks." The room fell silent and the whirling stopped. The young man's chest felt cold as his stomach returned to its natural position. He raised his eyes to the two officers sitting across from him. Both had a sneer on their lips.

"That's right," Walter said quietly. "That's exactly what happened," he said, recalling the beautiful Sunday afternoon and the tram trip back from the Grand Avenue Pier.

"Be more careful with the mail from now on, kid," one of the inspectors stated as he stood up and opened the door. "Get out of here."

It took everything Walter had not to stand up and flee the small office. He walked back down the corridor to his work station, suppressing the impulse to find a waste basket to vomit into; he could feel the postal inspectors' eyes on the back of his head as he walked back into the sorting room. He sat down carefully, finding his position at his workstation; his coworkers continued sorting the mail discreetly, as if they hadn't noticed his return. When he looked up at them a few seconds later, he noticed their sidelong glances and locked gazes with them, greeting their wide, inquisitive eyes with a smirk typical of Walter Disney's sense of humour. This smirk relieved the tension, and their day of work and joking resumed as before the grilling began.

Unfortunately for the young postman, his job at the Chicago Post Office was fraught with further drama, some of which proved tragic. Walter had just returned from his route to the post office, which was located in downtown Chicago's Federal Building, on the afternoon of Wednesday, September 4, 1918. He exited the post office located just off the rotunda of the Federal Building after dropping off his mailbag just after 3 p.m. An explosion shook the building as he walked over the pristine marble floor of the lobby, preceded by a loud FOOOOOM. Dust rained down from the West Adams Street entrance, filling the room. After being knocked to the ground by the blast, a bewildered Walter found himself rising up a few seconds later. Looking around, he spotted others crossing the rotunda in the same manner. Walter was perplexed when he noticed a woman walking nearby in a white dress was now wearing black; later, he realised her clothing had been coloured by the dust and smoke from the explosion.

Screams appeared to echo all around, accentuated by the eight-story dome that capped the foyer. Another young man was assisting an elderly woman, whose spectacles were glassless and hung crooked from her ears. Across the lobby, a large woman yelled that she had "lost all her money." Tattered bits of cloth, including sections of skirts and blouses, were strewn across the now dust-covered floor.

Hundreds of people began running towards the doors, as well as the now-defunct West Adams Street entrance. The flow of people came to a halt as on- and off-duty police officers blocked exits and shut doors in an attempt to discover those guilty of the explosion. Walter stood in line, trying not to lose his cool as he waited his turn to depart the building. After a lengthy exchange with the officers stationed outside the building, he staggered into the street, over the mounds of bricks and shattered wood. He barely noticed the sound of crushing glass beneath his feet as he walked away from the structure and onto the pavement across from the Federal structure. As his fears settled, he witnessed how glass shards seemed to blanket the roadway and walkways, as the powerful explosion had destroyed windows as high as five floors on either side of West Adams roadway. The propaganda posters inviting Americans to buy war bonds and enlist in the military were shredded and billowing in the breeze caused by individuals fleeing the scene.

Things were more hectic outside the Federal Building than within. Both men's and women's screams filled the air. People were stunned and sat on the ground or spread out in the street. A priest dressed in black moved amid the victims, caring to the injured and performing final rites for the dead and dying. A young woman's body lay beside the Federal Building, part of her skull torn off. Those close were shocked to find her still breathing, and even more shocked to witness the next few minutes as her respiration became shallower and then ceased. The sound of heavy cloth being dragged over the pavement added to the crying that filled the streets, as many eyes turned to the building's damaged entrance. A man was dragging a body down the stairs dressed in a shredded postal worker's outfit; the odd movement of the body led many to believe that every bone had been smashed. Walter was saddened to learn later that the murderer was William Wheeler, a 45-year-old coworker who delivered mail like him. As eyes turned to the ruckus, the sound of rapid horses' feet chopped down the road. A lone postal horse was limping down West Adams Street towards a police officer who was examining the devastation. He seized the horse's bite in an attempt to keep it from racing away. The horse's eyes were wide in panic as blood streamed down the side of its face. The police officer and others nearby watched as the furious animal dropped to the ground and died after being stopped.

As medical assistance neared, the clanging of ambulance bells could be heard in the distance. Hope soared for those standing in the rubble surrounding the Federal Building, but it was dashed when the ambulance bells were silenced by the sound of a crash. The ambulance, which was rushing to the scene of the explosion, had collided with the tail of a tram that had stopped to allow the ambulance to pass, wounding the two physicians and two patrolmen on board.

Walter, finally able to gather himself to make his journey home, gazed at the clock displayed on the corner of the Federal Building. The explosion had brought it to a halt at exactly 3.12 p.m. When he returned home, his mother and father expressed satisfaction that he had survived relatively unhurt.

Details regarding the explosion continued to surface over the next few days. An unnamed woman had just finished purchasing war stamps at the post office on the first floor of the Federal Building, located right inside the West Adams Street entrance, according to an article on page one of The Chicago Tribune. She observed a man waiting in the doorway with a cigar box under his arm and a piece of string dangling from beneath the box's cover. He allegedly took the cigar he was smoking and put the burning end of it to the string before dropping the box to the ground and kicking it beneath a nearby radiator before fleeing the premises, according to her. When the explosion happened, she was walking away from the entrance and across the lobby towards the Dearborn Street entrance of the building, which she found peculiar but not disturbing. While her story was not corroborated by other witnesses, a number of others reported seeing a short man, weighing about 65 kg and wearing a fedora or Panama hat made of brown felt, sprint out of the West Adams Street entrance and into a waiting car, which sped away just before the explosion.

William D. was eight storeys above the mayhem. 'Big Bill' Haywood was in a meeting with prosecutors, US marshals, and US officials. The Court of Appeal. Haywood founded and led the Industrial Workers of the World (commonly known as the I.W.W. or 'Wobblies'), a radical socialist-leaning labour union that advocated class warfare through strikes, boycotts, and industrial sabotage. Many of the I.W.W.'s tactics were aggressive and unlawful, resulting in several arrests. In 1917, Haywood and other leaders of the organisation were jailed for evading the American draft and encouraging a number of Chicago industrial workers to refuse to work, harming the wartime industry that supported American troops overseas. The American Espionage Act, which made it a criminal act for people within the United States to obstruct the war effort or aid any enemies of the United States, both internal and external, was cited by law enforcement agents from both the city of Chicago and the United States.

Haywood was upstairs meeting with representatives of the United States on the day of the explosion in Chicago's Federal Building. The Court of Appeals granted bond release from their 20-year sentence for members of the I.W.W. arrested under the Espionage Act. When the explosion shook the building, everyone in the room was lifted out of their chairs or hurled to the ground. A deputy marshal, Thomas Dolan, was astounded to see Haywood still in his chair, tapping a pencil against the table and staring out into space.

"They've bombed the place!"" yelled Dolan. Ms Mary Service, Haywood's private secretary, dashed to a nearby window and gazed down at the road below. Dolan and another deputy marshal, Fred Klika, rushed into the corridor, summoning one of the guards who had followed Haywood from the county jail that morning, who was also getting himself up from the floor.

After ordering the guard to keep a watch on the I.W.W. The two marshals gathered their colleagues and devised a strategy to round up other members of the organisation's leadership, thinking that the attack was the result of Haywood's appeal plea. While Dolan and Klika devised their strategy, Haywood calmed down, explaining to the guard and Mary Service that the explosion had nothing to do with the International Workers of the World.

"It could have been a German outrage," he continued, implying that the explosion was an attack by America's adversaries in the big war going on elsewhere. "It's a terrible thing to happen. No I.W.W. members would be so stupid as to do such a thing. "I am convinced that no member of the organisation was involved in this atrocity."

Top members of the I.W.W. leadership were apprehended during the next few hours. Raids were carried out on the organisation's two headquarters, resulting in the arrest of around 100 Wobblies. Numerous people were detained based on circumstantial evidence of items in their possession. For example, one suspect, James Connelly, was detained and charged with being involved in the attacks because he had a small lamp and receipts from an explosives firm in his pockets. Kent Rudin, another young guy, was arrested after being found reading I.W.W. literature. During his arrest, he was discovered to be carrying a corroded pistol, making him appear to be a "dangerous man." However, none of those apprehended 'in connection' with the Federal Building attack matched the description given by witnesses of the short man wearing the brown felt hat.

As the dust settled and cleanup began, it was revealed that the explosion had killed four people: in addition to Walter's colleague, William Wheeler, another postman named Edwin Kolkow, a young serviceman named Joseph Ladd, and the young woman with the head injury, Ella Miehlke. Seventy-five people were hurt in varying degrees by the explosion, whether from the shock of the bomb, flying debris, or falling glass. In an effort to protect 'Big Bill,' he was escorted down a service elevator to the ground floor, where he was handcuffed and brought to the county prison under heavy supervision. In 1919, a woman in Milwaukee, Wisconsin accused her husband, Dominick Costerella, of carrying out the Chicago Federal Building explosion as well as an attack on the Milwaukee Police Station in 1917 that killed ten people. When authorities finally apprehended Costerella, he was arrested in Pennsylvania on the same charges as his wife. After learning of his detention, his wife went to the police and revealed she made up the narrative in order to find her husband, who had abandoned her and vanished. Unfortunately, with the discovery that Mrs. Costerella's claim was fraudulent, the investigation of the United States Marshals and the Chicago Police came to a standstill, and most of those detained in the raids on the I.W.W. headquarters were freed after brief interrogation. After being released on bail during the appeals process in 1921, William Haywood escaped to Russia, where he died in 1928.

Chapter Twelve: Camp Scott

Elias and Flora Disney, initially unaware of their son's actual activities, believed he was aiding the American Red Cross stateside. However, Walter Disney didn't correct their misunderstanding, benefiting from their ignorance. He trained at Camp Scott,

Washington Park, where he and Russell were introduced to the camp's amenities and training program, including automotive repair and driving skills. Despite being underage, Walter managed to submit a passport application with altered details, ensuring his participation in the Red Cross.

During his training, Walter encountered the Spanish flu, falling ill but recovering at home. Despite missing his unit's departure for Europe due to his illness, Walter eventually joined another unit and was transferred to Camp King, Greenwich. His attitude became withdrawn, focusing on sketching rather than socialising. However, with the war's end and the signing of the Armistice, Walter's chance to serve overseas seemed lost until he was unexpectedly chosen to travel to France, fulfilling his long-held desire to make a difference.

Chapter Thirteen: The American Red Cross

While initially remaining neutral in the European battle, the United States assisted the Allies by providing medical relief and mobility services through various volunteer organisations. The American Field Service, for example, arrived in Europe in 1915, running sixty ambulances to take the wounded and dying to field hospitals beyond the front lines. More volunteer relief organisations, including the American Red Cross, the Knights of Columbus, and the Young Men's Christian Association, would arrive in Europe over the next few years to assist the American Field Service in caring for Allied wounded.

As soon as the aggressors declared war on one another in late summer 1914, the American Red Cross began mobilising to offer critical assistance to all wartime belligerents, including the Germans and Austro-Hungarians. Henry P. Davidson, director of the American Red Cross, believed that only by giving medical help would the world be brought back to peace: "[O]ur job in the American Red Cross," he went on to say, "is to bind up the wounds of a bleeding world...[and] succour wounded nations." As a result of this belief, on September 12, 1914, a ship called The Red Cross, nicknamed 'The Mercy Ship,' set sail from New York City for

Europe's war-ravaged and bloodied battlefields, carrying 170 surgeons and nurses organised into eleven units that would provide relief to each of the aggressor nations fighting in the war.

The American Red Cross provided medical help to Europe for the following thirteen months, from Britain to Serbia. However, medical teams were withdrawn from European battlefields in October 1915 because British officials were concerned that medical supplies utilised by the American Red Cross might fall into the hands of the Central Powers and be hoarded as an additional technique of assault against its opponents. Instead, the relief organisation began to fund the 130 other groups around the continent that supplied relief services to the aggressors.

The United States officially entered the war on the side of the Allies in 1917, allowing it to provide further services through the United States Army Ambulance Service, a division of the United States Army Medical Department. Because of backing from the US Army and the American federal government, this was far better equipped than the voluntary organisations. The Ambulance Service employed over 350,000 people, including over 21,000 nurses and 31,000 physicians, which equated to 24% of all doctors in the United States.

The United States Army's medical section used forty-six ambulances adapted by American automakers such as Ford and General Motors to meet the harsh wartime conditions of the European battlefields. According to a report filed by the United States Army Medical Department in 1925, Ford's Model T was easily able to navigate the high-grade roads of Western Europe and was light enough to be lifted by three or four troops should the vehicle become stuck in a shell hole on the battlefield.

In addition, the United States Army Medical Department created 152 base hospitals and over 100 camp hospitals to treat both American and Allied soldiers injured on the Western Front. To deal with the large number of patients arriving at hospitals, as well as those suffering from illnesses such as the Spanish flu, the medical service began to triage patients upon arrival, designating them as either requiring immediate care, providing comfort to those who were not expected to survive their injuries, or requiring services that could be delayed for a few days if necessary. In reality, the United States Army Medical Department immediately adopted the policy of performing as few procedures as possible on patients requiring delayed care at field hospitals in order to save as many beds and resources as possible for those requiring acute or end-of-life care. Those with non-urgent battlefield injuries or illnesses were instead loaded onto medical trains and transported to evacuation hospitals near Paris or other areas away from the front.

The United States Army Medical Department and its numerous branches, such as the Army Ambulance Service and the Sanitation Service, were immediately overwhelmed in providing relief not just to American troops but also to Allied troops. President Woodrow Wilson urged that the American Red Cross began mobilisation and fundraising for its war operations within the first month of American involvement. By August, the American Red Cross had developed an official policy regarding its involvement on the battlefields across the Atlantic: in terms of providing medical assistance to the wounded, the American Red Cross' neutrality ended in February 1917, at the same time as official American neutrality. They did, however, add that if they came across a wounded soldier lying on the battlefield, they "would not recognize the ethnicity of the wounded," allowing the American Red Cross to offer healthcare to everybody, ally and enemy alike. Not only did the relief organisation vow to provide help and assistance to civilian populations, but it also agreed to collaborate with other organisations delivering aid to war-torn nations, such as the Y.M.C.A., Jewish Welfare Board, Society of Friends, and Salvation Army. During the period when the American Red Cross aided the Allies during World War I, more than 91,000 people were treated in makeshift hospitals in France alone.

Members of the American Red Cross, the United States Army Medical Department, and other volunteer organisations involved in providing aid throughout the war faced peril. Ambulance drivers and medical professionals who gave support to troops on the front lines were continuously at risk and had to wear earplugs to protect their eardrums and goggles to prevent gunpowder and dust from seeping into their eyes. Some trench injuries were so severe that surgery and treatments had to be performed in the back of vehicles only metres from the battle, with shells exploding all around. In other situations, ambulances carrying wounded people fleeing the dangers of war were hit by explosions, bounced through shell holes, and were riddled with bullet wounds. Approximately 300 American Red Cross nurses and more than 120 ambulance drivers were killed as a result of this violence, and hundreds more were injured. Author Ernest Hemingway, whose leg was filled with shrapnel following an explosion, carried an injured soldier out of harm's way while rendering aid in Italy. The value of American medical personnel and ambulance drivers was recognized by Western and Central European governments; while the French government awarded the Croix de Guerre to the most heroic members of the American medical service, the Italian government decorated all American ambulance drivers for their role in providing aid and relief to civilians and soldiers alike.

During the conflict, the United States government and the United States conflict Department recognized the importance of troop and civilian morale. General John J. Pershing, commander of the American Expeditionary Forces on the Western Front, recognized the value of local morale when he directed Major Grayson M.P. Murphy, European Commissioner of the American Red Cross, to "buck up the French...[as] the value of the service [to Americans and foreign governments] is beyond computation...Nobody knows what will happen to us if they are not taken care of." The American Red Cross assisted local populations by rebuilding war-damaged homes, providing seed to farmers whose crops had been destroyed, constructing and operating orphanages for children whose parents were killed in the conflict, and establishing convalescent homes for those recovering from war-related injuries or illnesses such as the Spanish influenza epidemic. According to French general Marshal Philippe Pétain, "nothing has contributed more to the morale of my soldiers...[than] the American Red Cross in France."

In addition to providing medical care, relief, and help to the sick and injured, as well as relief and work to local citizens, the American Red Cross was supposed to 'offer recreational, educational, and religious programs for troops' in collaboration with the many relief organisations. The American Red Cross Canteen Service, which operated 130 canteens inside military camps, American Red Cross hospitals, and train stations along critical routes throughout France, would be in charge of this. These canteens provided a variety of amenities vital to the care and morale of American troops operating overseas, such as dormitories, restaurants selling free or reduced-price meals, lounging and leisure areas, bathrooms, barber shops, and even movie theatres.

During the war, the American Red Cross also provided services to Americans at home. Thousands of emergency American Red Cross nurses, aides, and volunteers were recruited to care for the extraordinary number of victims of the Spanish influenza outbreak. In February 1918, the American Red Cross Motor Service was founded, with 12,000 volunteers transporting sick and wounded personnel who had returned to the United States to evacuation facilities located on American Red Cross and military bases. The American Red Cross sponsored new organisations to provide services for the poor, such as occupational training programs for the blind, an institute for those who were crippled or disabled during the war, and a Sanitation Service, which ensured clean and sanitary conditions in large cities and areas affected by the Spanish flu. The American Red Cross also assisted families of American servicemen serving overseas by providing mortgage support, writing letters to families on behalf of injured and sick soldiers, and even investigating the fates of members who went missing or were killed in combat. On some occasions, the American Red Cross even photographed grave markers for soldiers who had been killed and buried overseas in order to provide closure to families.

The partnership between American civilians and the American Red Cross was mutually beneficial, not just for those at home. While fundraising activities helped the organisation raise much-needed funds, individuals also offered practical resources to support the hospitals and injured. For example, American women stitched and knitted about 23 million clothing, 300 million bandages, and 14 million medical supplies such as gowns and garments. They even helped the American Red Cross by stitching 1.4 million masks to aid in the relief of the Spanish flu outbreak. Hundreds of sewing circles each produced thousands of clothes in certain places, such as Chicago, where war fever was at its peak.

As American servicemen were brought home and relief organisations were disbanded following the Armistice, the American Red Cross found itself still playing an important role in the process of rebuilding a war-torn continent. Divisions were sent to dozens of countries to help war victims, such as providing milk and meals to orphaned children in Czechoslovakia, caring for those affected by the typhus epidemic in Poland and the Baltics where hospitals had been destroyed, operating relief stations and dispensaries in southeastern Europe, and even assisting in the reunification of refugee families in Russia. The organisation helped almost 1.7 million refugees in France by supplying food and clothing, repairing homes, and providing jobs and medical treatment. These services were provided until the individual governments were able to re-establish their own medical infrastructures, at which point labour and resources were moved to other countries or volunteers were repatriated back to the United States. Following the Russian Revolution and the rise of the Bolsheviks, the leadership of the American Red Cross decided, with the support of the US government, to withdraw their services from Russia, fearing that communist ideas would spread to the capitalist nations of Western Europe and America. By 1922, the American Red Cross had begun to withdraw its services, with the last volunteers returning to the United States a year later.

Overall, offering assistance to war victims, both fighters and civilians, was an important and honourable effort during and after the First World War. Henry Pomeroy Davison, Chairman of the American Red Cross War Council and creator of the League of Red Cross Societies, was entirely correct when he stated, "A contribution to the Red Cross [was] a contribution toward victory." Without the American Red Cross, or the American people who backed the voluntary aid organisation, Allied victory in Europe would not have been ensured.

Chapter Fourteen: France

After a journey on the SS Vauban from New Jersey to France, Walter Disney and his American Red Cross colleagues experienced various adventures during World War I. In France, they faced challenges like finding sleeping arrangements on the ship, navigating treacherous waters, and adjusting to cultural differences. Walter was assigned to sleep above the ship's magazine, adding excitement to his journey. The ship carried both relief workers and commercial cargo, creating logistical challenges. In France, they encountered makeshift minesweepers and navigated through Cherbourg Harbour's protective measures. Despite intending to disembark in Cherbourg, they were delayed due to cargo decisions and eventually reached Le Havre, where they stayed at a luxurious hotel and explored the city. Language barriers led to amusing situations, like misunderstanding the local restroom customs. Walter then travelled to Paris and Saint-Cyr, where he worked at an evacuation hospital and faced hardships like cold weather and limited resources. His artistic talents were recognized, and he used them to earn money and entertain colleagues. He also faced challenges like a court martial for a truck incident, which he overcame. Eventually, Walter returned to the U.S., but found his plans and expectations altered by circumstances and personal changes.

PART VI: I WANT TO BE AN ARTIST – KANSAS CITY, MISSOURI, 1919–1923

Chapter Fifteen: Advertising

While initially remaining neutral in the European battle, the United States assisted the Allies by providing medical relief and mobility services through various volunteer organisations. The American Field Service, for example, arrived in Europe in 1915, running sixty ambulances to take the wounded and dying to field hospitals beyond the front lines. More volunteer relief organisations, including the American Red Cross, the Knights of Columbus, and the Young Men's Christian Association, would arrive in Europe over the next few years to assist the American Field Service in caring for Allied wounded.

As soon as the aggressors declared war on one another in late summer 1914, the American Red Cross began mobilising to offer critical assistance to all wartime belligerents, including the Germans and Austro-Hungarians. Henry P. Davidson, director of the American Red Cross, believed that only by giving medical help would the world be brought back to peace: "[O]ur job in the American Red Cross," he went on to say, "is to bind up the wounds of a bleeding world...[and] succour wounded nations." As a result of this belief, on September 12, 1914, a ship called The Red Cross, nicknamed 'The Mercy Ship,' set sail from New York City for Europe's war-ravaged and bloodied battlefields, carrying 170 surgeons and nurses organised into eleven units that would provide relief to each of the aggressor nations fighting in the war.

The American Red Cross provided medical help to Europe for the following thirteen months, from Britain to Serbia. However, medical teams were withdrawn from European battlefields in October 1915 because British officials were concerned that medical supplies utilised by the American Red Cross might fall into the hands of the Central Powers and be hoarded as an additional technique of assault against its opponents. Instead, the relief organisation began to fund the 130 other groups around the continent that supplied relief services to the aggressors.

The United States officially entered the war on the side of the Allies in 1917, allowing it to provide further services through the United States Army Ambulance Service, a division of the United States Army Medical Department. Because of backing from the US Army and the American federal government, this was far better equipped than the voluntary organisations. The Ambulance Service employed over 350,000 people, including over 21,000 nurses and 31,000 physicians, which equated to 24% of all doctors in the United States.

The United States Army's medical section used forty-six ambulances adapted by American automakers such as Ford and General Motors to meet the harsh wartime conditions of the European battlefields. According to a report filed by the United States Army Medical Department in 1925, Ford's Model T was easily able to navigate the high-grade roads of Western Europe and was light enough to be lifted by three or four troops should the vehicle become stuck in a shell hole on the battlefield.

In addition, the United States Army Medical Department created 152 base hospitals and over 100 camp hospitals to treat both American and Allied soldiers injured on the Western Front. To deal with the large number of patients arriving at hospitals, as well as those suffering from illnesses such as the Spanish flu, the medical service began to triage patients upon arrival, designating them as either requiring immediate care, providing comfort to those who were not expected to survive their injuries, or requiring services that could be delayed for a few days if necessary. In reality, the United States Army Medical Department immediately adopted the policy of performing as few procedures as possible on patients requiring delayed care at field hospitals in order to save as many beds and resources as possible for those requiring acute or end-of-life care. Those with non-urgent combat injuries or illnesses were instead placed onto medical trains and taken to evacuation hospitals near Paris or other regions away from the front.

The United States Army Medical Department and its numerous branches, such as the Army Ambulance Service and the Sanitation Service, were immediately overwhelmed in providing relief not just to American troops but also to Allied troops. President Woodrow

Wilson urged that the American Red Cross began mobilisation and fundraising for its war operations within the first month of American involvement. By August, the American Red Cross had developed an official policy regarding its involvement on the battlefields across the Atlantic: in terms of providing medical assistance to the wounded, the American Red Cross' neutrality ended in February 1917, at the same time as official American neutrality. They did, however, add that if they came across a wounded soldier lying on the battlefield, they "would not recognize the ethnicity of the wounded," allowing the American Red Cross to offer healthcare to everybody, ally and enemy alike. Not only did the relief organisation vow to provide help and assistance to civilian populations, but it also agreed to collaborate with other organisations delivering aid to war-torn nations, such as the Y.M.C.A., Jewish Welfare Board, Society of Friends, and Salvation Army. During the period when the American Red Cross aided the Allies during World War I, more than 91,000 people were treated in makeshift hospitals in France alone.

Members of the American Red Cross, the United States Army Medical Department, and other volunteer organisations involved in providing aid throughout the war faced peril. Ambulance drivers and medical professionals who gave support to troops on the front lines were continuously at risk and had to wear earplugs to protect their eardrums and goggles to prevent gunpowder and dust from seeping into their eyes. Some trench injuries were so severe that surgery and treatments had to be performed in the back of vehicles only metres from the battle, with shells exploding all around. In other situations, ambulances carrying wounded people fleeing the dangers of war were hit by explosions, bounced through shell holes, and were riddled with bullet wounds. Approximately 300 American Red Cross nurses and more than 120 ambulance drivers were killed as a result of this violence, and hundreds more were injured. Author Ernest Hemingway, whose leg was filled with shrapnel following an explosion, carried an injured soldier out of harm's way while rendering aid in Italy. The value of American medical personnel and ambulance drivers was recognized by Western and Central European governments; while the French government awarded the Croix de Guerre to the most heroic members of the American medical service, the Italian government decorated all American ambulance drivers for their role in providing aid and relief to civilians and soldiers alike.

During the conflict, the United States government and the United States conflict Department recognized the importance of troop and civilian morale. General John J. Pershing, commander of the American Expeditionary Forces on the Western Front, recognized the value of local morale when he directed Major Grayson M.P. Murphy, European Commissioner of the American Red Cross, to "buck up the French...[as] the value of the service [to Americans and foreign governments] is beyond computation...Nobody knows what will happen to us if they are not taken care of." The American Red Cross assisted local populations by rebuilding war-damaged homes, providing seed to farmers whose crops had been destroyed, constructing and operating orphanages for children whose parents were killed in the conflict, and establishing convalescent homes for those recovering from war-related injuries or illnesses such as the Spanish influenza epidemic. According to French general Marshal Philippe Pétain, "nothing has contributed more to the morale of my soldiers...[than] the American Red Cross in France."

In addition to providing medical care, relief, and help to the sick and injured, as well as relief and work to local citizens, the American Red Cross was supposed to 'offer recreational, educational, and religious programs for troops' in collaboration with the many relief organisations. The American Red Cross Canteen Service, which operated 130 canteens inside military camps, American Red Cross hospitals, and train stations along critical routes throughout France, would be in charge of this. These canteens provided a variety of amenities vital to the care and morale of American troops operating overseas, such as dormitories, restaurants selling free or reduced-price meals, lounging and leisure areas, bathrooms, barber shops, and even movie theatres.

During the war, the American Red Cross also provided services to Americans at home. Thousands of emergency American Red Cross nurses, aides, and volunteers were recruited to care for the extraordinary number of victims of the Spanish influenza outbreak. In February 1918, the American Red Cross Motor Service was founded, with 12,000 volunteers transporting sick and wounded personnel who had returned to the United States to evacuation facilities located on American Red Cross and military bases. The American Red Cross sponsored new organisations to provide services for the poor, such as occupational training programs for the blind, an institute for those who were crippled or disabled during the war, and a Sanitation Service, which ensured clean and sanitary conditions in large cities and areas affected by the Spanish flu. The American Red Cross also assisted families of American servicemen serving overseas by providing mortgage support, writing letters to families on behalf of injured and sick soldiers, and even investigating the fates of members who went missing or were killed in combat. On some occasions, the American Red Cross even photographed grave markers for soldiers who had been killed and buried overseas in order to provide closure to families.

The partnership between American civilians and the American Red Cross was mutually beneficial, not just for those at home. While fundraising activities helped the organisation raise much-needed funds, individuals also offered practical resources to support the hospitals and injured. For example, American women stitched and knitted about 23 million clothing, 300 million bandages, and 14 million medical supplies such as gowns and garments. They even helped the American Red Cross by stitching 1.4 million masks to aid in the relief of the Spanish flu outbreak. Hundreds of sewing circles each produced thousands of clothes in certain places, such as Chicago, where war fever was at its peak.

As American servicemen were brought home and relief organisations were disbanded following the Armistice, the American Red Cross found itself still playing an important role in the process of rebuilding a war-torn continent. Divisions were sent to dozens of countries to help war victims, such as providing milk and meals to orphaned children in Czechoslovakia, caring for those affected by the typhus epidemic in Poland and the Baltics where hospitals had been destroyed, operating relief stations and dispensaries in southeastern Europe, and even assisting in the reunification of refugee families in Russia. The organisation helped almost 1.7 million refugees in France by supplying food and clothing, repairing homes, and providing jobs and medical treatment. These services were provided until the individual governments were able to re-establish their own medical infrastructures, at which point labour and resources were moved to other countries or volunteers were repatriated back to the United States. Following the Russian Revolution and the rise of the Bolsheviks, the leadership of the American Red Cross decided, with the support of the US government, to withdraw their services from Russia, fearing that communist ideas would spread to the capitalist nations of Western Europe and America. By 1922, the American Red Cross had begun to withdraw its services, with the last volunteers returning to the United States a year later.

Overall, offering assistance to war victims, both fighters and civilians, was an important and honourable effort during and after the First World War. Henry Pomeroy Davison, Chairman of the American Red Cross War Council and creator of the League of Red Cross Societies, was entirely correct when he stated, "A contribution to the Red Cross [was] a contribution toward victory." Without the American Red Cross, or the American people who backed the voluntary aid organisation, Allied victory in Europe would not have been ensured.

Chapter Sixteen: Early Animation

In 1920, Walt Disney began working at Cauger's Kansas City Slide Company (later Kansas City Film Ad Company), learning animation techniques. He declined a job offer from The Kansas City Journal, preferring his role at Cauger's. The company, struggling with inconsistent work, eventually failed, buy Disney secured a position for his friend Ubbe Iwwerks there. They advanced in animated advertising and studied Eadweard Muybridge's book "Animals in Motion" for better animation techniques.

Meanwhile, advancements in motion pictures were made globally, with Muybridge's zoopraxiscope, Edison's Kinetoscope, Reynaud's praxinoscope, and Lumière brothers' film projector, leading to the birth of Nickelodeons and the rise of animation.

Disney's Laugh-O-Grams gained popularity, leading to a contract with the Newman Theater Company. Disney's innovative techniques and artistic growth allowed him to start his own studio. Personal challenges, including his brother Roy's health and family relocation, influenced Disney's focus on his career. As the sole Disney family member in Missouri, he continued to innovate in animation, laying the groundwork for his future success.

Chapter Seventeen: Laugh-O-gram

Walt was the only Disney still living in Kansas City, and the Bellefontaine mansion had been sold, so he was without a place to live and had to fend for himself. He'd lately moved in with Dr. John Cowles and his young family: Dr. Cowles had been the Disneys' family physician for years and had formed a close relationship with them. Walt soon after moved into an apartment on adjacent Charlotte Street. To avoid loneliness, the young man resolved to occupy his time with employment. Walt was hired by Pathé Newsreel, Selznick News, and the Universal Film Manufacturing Company to produce newsreels in Kansas City, using the Universal camera he'd purchased with his earnings from the Kansas City Film Ad Company. When he wasn't working, Walt would walk around town with his camera, looking for important occurrences to record and send back to Hollywood for inclusion in Universal's newsreels.

One of the more significant events captured by Walt was the groundbreaking of the Liberty Memorial, which is located in downtown Kansas City across from Union Station. The groundbreaking was conducted on November 1, 1921, in preparation of the memorial's unveiling on November 11, 1926, the eighth anniversary of the signing of the Armistice. In addition to the hundreds of thousands of Kansas Citians who attended the ceremony, President Calvin Coolidge, Marshal Foch of France, General Pershing of the United States, General Diaz of Italy, Admiral Lord Beatty of Britain, and Lieutenant General Jacques of Belgium were all invited to participate in the day's events, marking the first time all five Allied commanders had appeared together in public.

Walt opted to take a different method to collecting the footage because he couldn't get close enough to record the event in full. Walt ascended onto the roof of a building overlooking the Kansas City Star building, where Coolidge, Foch, and Pershing sat in a reviewing stand, while a military parade moved down Grand Boulevard towards Union Station. Walt was able to obtain footage of both the parade going southbound and the formidable trio enjoying the entertainment by craneing his camera.

Walt had also heard that several WWI pilots would be performing aerial stunts over the city. While most people were used to watching air shows from the ground, the young filmmaker wanted the newsreel viewers to feel as if they were in the dogfight and had secured a seat aboard one of the planes. Walt sought advice from another photographer, who advised him to reduce the size of the lens aperture: this would reduce the amount of light entering the camera, allowing for greater dimension in the film.

When it was time for the show to begin, Walt joined the pilot and Hugh Harman's younger brother, Fred, in the cockpit of the First World War plane. Walt, who was sitting on Harman's knee, stood up and pointed the camera at the other planes executing tricks as the plane took off. Harman remained seated, holding the tripod firm so the camera didn't fall over.

Walt's voice was lost in the bluster of the wind as he began to call down to Harman that he was going to start turning the camera. Their gazes locked as Walt gestured what he was about to do, and Harman nodded to indicate that he understood. The two young filmmakers were blown away by the action they observed and captured, which included barrel rolls and loop-the-loops performed by the planes.

Walt jumped onto the runway when the plane finished its antics, seizing the camera from Harman as he handed it down. "Boy!"He practically jumped," he cried. "They're going to buy it!" Perhaps they'll even offer us a raise!"Walt received the processed film a few weeks later. He gathered his animators and Fred Harman from the Kansas City Film Ad Company, loaded the film into a projector, and played it. He was devastated to see that it only showed a grey background with a whirling black object flickering across it. He soon realised the film only showed the aeroplane propeller. A jolt rattled the film and the screen went blank, prompting him to realise he had set the aperture too low, allowing insufficient light to reach the lens. His footage was a failure.

Recognizing that he should stick to what he understood best, Walt handed Cougar his notice in early 1922, stating that he had decided to focus on developing Laugh-O-Grams and other short animated pictures for Newman full-time. While Cougar was obviously disappointed to lose one of his finest painters, he recognized that this was where Walt's true talent and passion lay and sent him on his way with best wishes.

Walt quickly went out to raise funds to fund his new enterprise. He was no longer utilising the garage he'd built with Elias as his makeshift studio now that the Bellefontaine house had been sold to a new family. Over the next few months, Walt leveraged his appeal to attract investments from a variety of community members, including Dr. Cowles and his wife Minnie. It was especially beneficial when Frank Newman learned of Walt's financial needs and volunteered to play one of the Laugh-O-gram pictures in his theatre to attract investors. Several people soon bought shares in Laugh-O-gram, with several owning between $250 and $500 worth of stock. By May 1922, Walt had acquired more than $15,000 in funding, enough to establish a new film production firm. Walt Disney officially founded Laugh-O-gram on May 23, 1922, omitting Newman as the prefix because he hoped to distribute to a wider audience than only those who patronised Newman-owned theatres.

Walt chose to expand his workforce with the newly gained money investments as they poured themselves into the construction of their newest venture: sketching modern-day versions of fairy tales. Walt soon had a staff of eleven people, including newcomers Carman Maxwell, Lorey Tague, Otto Walliman, Walt Pfeiffer, camera operator Red Lyon, distribution salesman Leslie Mace, stenographer/bookkeeper Nadine Simpson, and Aletha Reynolds, who was in charge of tracing and inking the artists' sketches onto celluloid for photographing.

When Little Red Riding Hood was finished in May 1922, Mace was dispatched to New York, where distributors for animated shorts were based, to locate someone interested in distributing Laugh-O-Grams to theatres around the country. While Mace was unable to identify anyone from the major film studios interested in the animated fairy tales, he was referred to William R. Kelley, a representative of Pictorial Clubs Incorporated's Tennessee division, a company that distributed pictures to schools and churches. While this was less than ideal, Walt saw it as an open door that may lead to better things and told his salesman to sign a deal on September 16. The deal asked for a total of six animated shorts and called for a total payment of $11,100 for the series, with the studio receiving a $100 advance upon signing the contract and the rest $11,000 payable by January 24, 1924. Walt saw the deal with Pictorial Clubs as an opportunity to attract Ubbe Iwwerks to Laugh-O-gram, and Ubbe quickly abandoned his job at the Kansas City Film Ad Company to join the developing organisation in their new enterprise.

Walt thought that the Laugh-O-gram personnel needed somewhere more official to work in making their animated shorts with their investments, incorporation, and the promise of thousands of cash from Pictorial Clubs. Walt was drawn to a new structure at the intersection of 31st Street and Forest Avenue in southeast Kansas City, just a few kilometres from the Bellefontaine residence. The McConahay Building was designed by Nelle E. Peters, a notable Kansas City architect who had already constructed a number of local hotels and apartment complexes, and was finished in 1922. When Laugh-O-gram moved in, it took over five rooms on the second story of the property, above a shoe store and restaurant called the Forest Inn Café.

The environment at Laugh-O-gram's studio was one of collaboration, joy, and companionship, more comparable to a fraternity than a company. The artists would frequently play practical jokes on each other or on unsuspecting Kansas City residents. In one case, the boys put a sign on their car identifying them as from a studio and mounted their camera on the back, attracting the attention of those nearby who wanted to be seen in newsreels that would be shown across America. At other times, they'd bring their camera to Union Station and stand in the Grand Hall or North Waiting Room, with Walt cranking the empty camera and the artists performing antics to the amusement of the public, who thought they were watching a movie being made. The artists also visited adjacent Swope Park, where they stayed in a log cabin in a wooded location.

Walt and his painters began work on their second animated fairy tale, The Four Musicians of Bremen, soon after moving into their new studio. This was swiftly followed by Jack and the Beanstalk, Goldie Locks and the Three Bears, Puss in Boots, and Cinderella, completing the list of films promised under Pictorial Clubs' contractual responsibilities.

These early animated fairy tales were generally characterised by jerky motions and sparse detail, particularly in the background. They also used time-saving techniques such as cycling and repeat action: for example, the first scene in The Four Musicians of Bremen included more than fifteen seconds of people throwing bricks and glass bottles at the film's main characters as they fled, with the same animations repeated every two seconds. This technique enabled less drawings to be created by capturing the same stills many times to lengthen a cartoon. Instead of spending time inventing fresh, distinctive characters, the team frequently recycled stock characters from one film to the next, so the same minor cat character may appear as an 'extra' in numerous Laugh-O-gram films. Despite their crudeness, these early works contained what made Disney films so famous to millions around the world over the past century: an integration of storyline and gags, witty humour, and likeable animal characters.

The company quickly developed short joke reels known as 'Lafflets,' allowing for experimenting with the burgeoning medium of film animation with a focus on hilarious jokes rather than plot. Disney's artists began to experiment with stop-motion, claymation, and animation using celluloid sheets (commonly known as cels), which they had previously used to create Jack and the Beanstalk for Pictorial Clubs. Walt began looking for a large studio distributor who could utilise the Lafflets as fillers between feature films and newsreels in theatres after combining these experimental pictures into a single reel. Unfortunately, there was little enthusiasm for this new offering.

There was no consistent income for Laugh-O-gram's work developing animated fairy tale shorts for Pictorial Clubs: the remaining $11,000 wouldn't be paid until the six contractual films were submitted. As a result, funds were frequently scarce, and Walt resorted to paying his artists in studio stock shares rather than cash. In addition, rather than paying for the services provided to the studio on a monthly basis, debts began to mount, which Walt planned to pay off once he received the final payment from Pictorial Clubs.

Unfortunately, this did not happen. Pictorial Clubs, Inc.'s Tennessee branch collapsed at the end of 1922. This meant that Laugh-O-gram's efforts on the six animated fairy tales had been in vain. Pictorial Clubs' New York branch absorbed the Tennessee branch, which meant that while the firm acquired the bankrupt company's assets, they refused to pay any of the bills owing. As a result, the New York branch refused to pay the agreed-upon $11,000 to Laugh-O-gram.

Walt began to scrounge up ideas for paying off debts accumulated over the preceding few months, including those owing to energy providers and retailers that sold supplies for the making of their films.

One afternoon, as the painters were hard at work, a man in a suit carrying a briefcase walked up the stairs and into the lobby of Laugh-O-gram.

"Does Mr Dinsey happen to be here?"" he inquired of Nadine Simpson, who sat at her desk near the stairwell. She turned to glance at Rudy Ising, who was sitting nearby, and then at Walt, who was working hard on the opposite side of the room.

"No, I don't think so," Walt replied, not looking up.

"Well, I'll be right back," the man said. As he moved back downstairs, the sound of his shoes faded, the door to the street opening and closing behind him.

"What?"Walt asked his staff, who had all come to a halt and stared at him. "He's clearly a debt collector looking for a Mr Dinsey." "No one by that name works here," he explained, smirking.

The collector visited several times more, each time mispronouncing Walt's name. Each time, Walt or one of his employees, who had learned to regard this as a harmless game, sent him away.

When the debt collector visited one afternoon, Walt was discussing a scene with Walt Pfeiffer. As they disagreed over a scenario, the collector stood at Simpson's desk, irritated that he'd missed 'Mr Dinsey' yet again.

Pfeiffer abruptly raised his voice. "Now listen, Walt..."

The debt collector's head turned to face them. "Walt?" he inquired. "Who is Walt Dinsey?""

"Yeah," Walt said, upset by his quarrel with Pfeiffer and the collector's continued failure. "It's me. However, it is pronounced Disney, not Disney."

The debt collector indicated that he needed to talk about account settlement with Walt, and the two moved into a corner and sat at an animation desk to look over papers. An agreement was reached on how the debts would be paid, but it immediately became clear that the funding required to continue producing animated shorts was low, and the chances of obtaining new contracts were slim. Some of Walt's artists left Laugh-O-gram to pursue other opportunities, including Ubbe, who returned to his job at the Kansas City Film Ad Company.

The majority of the investment funds he had received had been spent on producing the Laugh-O-Grams, so Walt had to dive into his own savings to pay off part of the studio's debts. It had to be decided whether to pay rent for his apartment on Charlotte Street or the Laugh-O-gram studios. Walt decided to keep the studio on 31st Street and left his apartment, preferring to reside at the studio. Despite the fact that sleeping in a desk chair was quite unpleasant, Walt never gave up on his dream, preferring to work and live in film animation.

Because the studio lacked a full bathing suite, Walt walked several kilometres each week to Union Station for a hot bath, where a dime got him a little cake of soap, a clean towel, and the opportunity to bathe in semi-private quarters. Walt felt discouraged when he came through the front doors of Union Station and observed well-dressed business people meeting beneath the giant clock. Walt was brought upstairs to enjoy his monthly bath after checking in at a little desk at Pierpont's, a waiting room for women and children located just off the Grand Hall. After that, he'd have a smoke in the men's smoking lounge or stroll through the doors of the North Waiting Room, where he'd stand on the train platforms, a wave of melancholy washing over him as he remembered Elias, Flora, and Ruth's departure for Portland.

Meals were mainly consumed at the studio, where Walt had begun eating unheated cans of chilli and beans because it was all he could afford. On special occasions, the homeless and hungry young man would walk downstairs to eat at the Forest Inn Café, where he had made friends with owners Louie Katsis and Jerry Raggos, who let him run up a tab in exchange for a promise to pay them back. This deal, however, came to an end when Walt's debt to the restaurant reached $60 and Katsis disconnected him. When Raggos went upstairs to get money to pay off the debt, he found Walt eating from a tin can in the middle of the vacant room. His annoyance quickly dissipated.

"Walt, I don't care what Louis says," Raggos stated as he approached him. "Come down to our place and have a bite to eat."

While he could take advantage of the kindness of the restaurant owners downstairs, Walt nevertheless felt quite alone; not only had his family left for the west, but his animators, including best friends Walt Pfeiffer and Ubbe Iwwerks, had given up on working for the company. Roy's fiancée, Edna Francis, still lived in Kansas City, and she frequently invited her boyfriend's little brother home for dinner and company, but this only made him feel better for a few hours before he returned to the cold darkness of the studio.

Walt was also fortunate in that, even though his former Laugh-O-gram workers had split ways professionally, some of them kept in touch. Nadine Simpson, Walt's former stenographer, rushed to his aid when she learned of his financial difficulties. Simpson discovered the grand prize of the lottery drawing was groceries and a ham while attending a church event. She immediately thought about her former boss and bought two $2 tickets. When one of her lottery tickets won, she presented the food to Walt, who was too nice to be humiliated.

Fortunately, Walt had made some studio friends: a few little mice who had been living off the crumbs of his leftover meals. When the studio was still a hive of activity, one of these mice began shuffling crumpled papers about inside a wire wastebasket, prompting Walt to discover him and warmly name him Mortimer. The studio head promptly adopted Mortimer and his pals as mascots, keeping them in a small cage on his desk during the day and storing them in one of his desk drawers at night.

Walt was able to supplement his income by working on local film projects. Dr. Thomas B. McCrum, a Kansas City dentist and the Deaner Dental Institute's director, learned about the local filmmaker in the early autumn of 1922. McCrum contacted Walt, and the two struck an agreement in which Walt would create an educational DVD for dentists about the importance of oral cleanliness. The short film, Tommy Tucker's Tooth, which included mostly live-action, earned Disney a $500 commission, which he used to pay off some of his obligations.

McCrum phoned Walt at the studio when it was time to sign out the contract and pay Walt the money for Tommy Tucker's Tooth.

"I have the funds for your film. "I'd like you to come to my office so we can finalise the arrangement," the dentist explained.

"I'm sorry, but I can't come over," Walt explained.

"What's the harm?"" McCrum inquired.

A hush fell across the line. "Well," the nervous young artist began. "My lone pair of sneakers were fraying. So I took them downstairs to the cobbler to be mended. The repair cost more than I expected, and he won't let me have them back until I cough up a dollar and a half."

"I'll be right over," McCrum assured her. The dentist had hung up the phone before Walt could object. Within an hour, Walt's new client was knocking on the studio door. Walt opened the door after walking down the shadowy staircase to the first floor in his stocking feet to discover Dr McCrum waiting on the pavement with Walt's shoes in hand: he had paid the cobbler what he was owed for the artist's repair work. After finishing up upstairs, Walt stepped into McCrum's car and drove to the dentist's office to sign the deal for the educational film.

Walt explored the neighbourhoods surrounding the Laugh-O-gram studio for children to fill the roles in his film, eventually selecting a young man named Jack Records as the lead actor and even filming at Benton Grammar School, where he had attended as a boy. Walt stood nearby, a cardboard megaphone in his hand and a cap on his head, advising the youngsters on what to do and say between takes. Walt's concept for the picture was clearly in his head, as none of the youngsters had been given a script to memorise. Instead, Walt would act out what he wanted the performers to do, start the camera, and shout out cues and movements while the children imitated Walt's performance.

While funds were scarce owing to a lack of work, Walt frequently paid the 5-cent entry to neighbourhood theatres to keep up with what the big animation studios in New York were doing. The teenage Walt Disney met Carl Stalling, a musician who played the theatre organ to accompany the silent action on screen, at the Isis Theater, about 120 metres from the Laugh-O-gram studio on the corner of 31st Street and Troost Avenue. Stalling stated to his friend that the Isis Theater planned to create a series of films dubbed 'Song-O-Reels,' in which the lyrics to a song would be projected beneath recorded action, encouraging viewers to sing along and serve as a filler between features and newsreels. Walt, who was short on finances, accepted the offer and began meeting with Isis Theater and J.W. Jenkins Music Company is a Kansas City-based music company.

It was determined that the first Song-O-Reel would complement Joe L. Sanders's newly-published song Martha: Just a Plain Old-Fashioned Name. Walt was granted creative licence to cast the characters as a filmmaker. Walt met his cast - some of the old Laugh-O-gram girls and Ubbe as their object of adoration - at Swope Park on the day of filming. While they had previously worked as equals on animated pictures, they now subordinated to Walt, the director giving direction, yelling out cues via megaphone, and demonstrating them their actions by miming them himself. However, much like Tommy Tucker's Tooth and the Lafflets, Martha was Walt's lone Song-O-Reel.

Unfortunately, none of these endeavours resulted in new opportunities for the budding artist. Walt saw that his local live-action work had been less successful than his animation efforts. He continued to visit theatres throughout Kansas City for inspiration, seeing what the big animation studios were doing.

After the conclusion of one of these cartoon shorts one day in early 1923, a still advertisement for Warneker's Bread flashed onto the screen. The advertisement, created by the Kansas City Film Ad Company, depicted a cheerful girl clutching a piece of jam-covered bread, with a speech bubble filled with the words, "Oh, yum, yum!" to one side."

As he sat in the dimly lit theatre, one of Walt's brows furrowed. He didn't notice when the next movie started, the low grey light flickering over his face. He had an idea, one that had never been tried before.

Chapter Eighteen: Bankruptcy

While animation was merely a novelty in the early years of the twentieth century, thanks to pioneers such as Émile Cohl, J. Stuart Blackton, and Winsor McCay, some innovations enabled films to be produced more quickly and cheaply, and more easily distributed to larger audiences across the country, eventually leading to the emergence of dedicated animation studios.

While early animators hand-drew each individual frame shot, it rapidly became clear that this was not the most effective method. On August 11, 1914, John Randolph Bray, the successful creator of one of the earliest animated shows, Colonel Heeza Liar, was granted the unique patent for the use of celluloid in animation. Bray had realised that he could sketch the scene's backdrops on translucent paper, with each new character movement on blank paper that could be seen through the background.

Earl Hurd, an artist, improved on Bray's approach a few months later by simply flipping the process: creating backgrounds on blank paper, with the characters and fresh animation on the thin, clear piece of celluloid that was placed over the top of the backdrop. Multiple layers of celluloid might be layered on top of each other, adding dimension to the scene. Hurd applied for and was granted a patent for this procedure on December 9, 1914.

Both Bray and Hurd's innovations considerably improved the process of animating. Rather than sketching the same backdrop thousands of times on various pieces of paper, as McCay had done, the background only needed to be drawn once, and the new animation was simply layered over the background on the cel. This made the entire animation process easier, faster, and less expensive, allowing for more animated shorts to be produced in less time.

This new technological breakthrough inspired those interested in animation to establish their own studios in New York, where the industry was centred in the 1910s and 1920s. When many of the big film studios moved their production west to Hollywood, the animation studios often stayed put: the creation of hand-drawn films wasn't reliant on the weather or landscape like live-action films were, and many of the film distributors were located in New York City due to their close relationship with the American business and financial world.

Several new animation companies formed throughout the 1910s, none of which survived long, but each of which made discoveries or technological advances that helped pave the way for the renowned studios that followed. Raoul Barré, the first major studio, was created in 1914 and invented the peg system, which kept blank pieces of paper on an animator's desk by a series of pegs located above the drawing surface. Artists could quickly layer their drawings in this manner, allowing them to flip between sketches to see whether the character had attained the appropriate degree of movement.

As these animation studios grew in size, a severe rivalry system arose. To compete with Hearst International, another prominent studio, Raoul Barré began to give art lessons for their animators, which included future Disney artists Dick Huemer, Bill Tytla, Albert Hurter, and Ted Sears, to ensure that figures had appropriate movements.

Another one of the studios is J.R. Bray followed in the footsteps of McCay's Gertie the Dinosaur by allowing their cartoons to violate the fourth wall. For example, in their 1915 syndicated series Bobby Bumps, the invisible animator interacted with the characters by creating items to help them get out of sticky situations. To fulfil Universal's growing demand for animated shorts, Bray implemented the animation assembly line system, which assigned artists to different positions within the company. While one person was fast sketching the characters on blank paper, another would be tracing the sketch with ink onto a piece of celluloid, and a third would be filling in the inked cell with paint to create varied hues and details on screen.

By the conclusion of the second decade of the twentieth century, newly created studios had surpassed Barré, Hearst, and Bray in popularity, technique, and quality. Pat Sullivan and Otto Messmer released Feline Follies in 1919, which was syndicated by Universal and marketed by Margaret Winkler in 1921. The short's protagonist, Felix the Cat, immediately became recognizable throughout America as Winkler collaborated with Sullivan to create a marketing campaign that included goods that fans of the naughty animal could purchase. Felix was also extremely popular with viewers because Sullivan and Messmer had given him a personality, which was novel in comparison to the dozens of emotionally bland characters that had preceded him on television. The humour in the Felix cartoons was also unique, because Felix frequently used his bodily parts, such as his tail, to assist him solve difficulties.

Sullivan and Messmer soon found a worthy competition in Max Fleischer's new animation studio. Fleischer, on the other hand, approached the medium in a different way than Sullivan and their forefathers. While many in the business focused on enhancing animation quality by developing new techniques, Fleischer focused on identifying new ways to use technology to improve animation. He was particularly fascinated in rotoscoping, which involves projecting live-action movies one frame at a time onto a blank piece of paper while an artist traced the figure and added his own details. This approach improved the fluidity and lifelike movement of animated figures, resulting in more viewer buy-in to the believability of an animated scenario.

Fleischer put his new technique to the test by creating the character Koko the Clown, played by his brother Dave. Fleischer added a clown outfit and make-up after copying Dave's body and gestures on sketch paper. Koko's movements were astonishingly realistic when projected on film as he swirled and jumped across the screen. Fleischer travelled to Hollywood in 1919, realising he had uncovered something extraordinary, to speak with Adolph Zukor, creator of Paramount Pictures. When he met John Bray in Zukor's outbuilding, he was fascinated by the artist's test reel of Koko and gave him a deal for Paramount to release one of Fleischer's reels every month as part of the Paramount Pictograph screen magazine. This association with Paramount continued until 1921, when Fleischer formed his own company, Out of the Inkwell Films, Inc., and teamed with Samuel Goldwyn.

Not only was Fleischer's animation method groundbreaking, but so were the cartoons' subjects. Each short in the 'Out of the Inkwell' series began with an image of Max Fleischer seated at his artist's desk. The artist began sketching Koko, who mysteriously came to life after dipping his pen in an inkwell. Koko would delight audiences throughout the shorts by fighting live-action flies that dropped on the paper, running away from ink blotters, or even leaping over the artist's desk and running about the live-action office or sliding down the leg of a chair. This approach of introducing the animated Koko into the live-action world was finished by using another technological process pioneered by Fleischer known as rotographing, which is the practice of overlaying an animation cel over a still frame of a photograph. The novelty of an animated figure interacting with real-world objects, people, and locations drew audiences in, but the animated pieces lacked logical narratives, instead relying on humour and two-dimensional characters.

Thus, the early 1920s cartoons that captivated and pleased audiences featured an animated clown who inserted himself into the actual world and a cat full of personality that exploited body parts to aid escape desperate situations. As a young Walt Disney sat in that darkened theatre, staring at the starving girl in the bread ad, he realised that if he wanted to break into the realm of animation, he needed to develop something new that would be equally as enticing to current audiences.

Virginia Davis was the small girl in the bread ad. The curly-haired, bright-eyed little girl was already a local figure on Kansas City theatre screens at 4 years old, thanks to her infrequent modelling work with the Kansas City Film Ad Company. Her parents wanted more for their little daughter than being featured in still advertisements, so they sent her to the Georgia Brown Dramatic School to polish her skills in singing, acting, and dancing.

Walt wrote to Mr. and Mrs. Davis after learning the girl's name from his contacts at the Kansas City Film Ad Company, asking if they would be interested in having their daughter star in his newest film. When he offered to pay Davis 5% of all profits from the film, they jumped at the chance, officially signing a deal with Walt on April 13, 1923.

Walt realised that this new project, Alice's Wonderland, might be his only shot to get into the animation industry and began to immerse himself into it. While his artists had abandoned him, he was able to persuade a few others, like Rudy Ising and Ubbe, to assist, with Ising running the camera, Ubbe producing most of the animation, and Walt directing the live-action parts.

The idea for Alice's Wonderland was simply the polar opposite of Fleischer's successful series. While audiences had been captivated by Koko the Clown's adventures in the real world, Walt bet that a real little girl finding herself in the cartoon world would pique their interest just as much. Walt Disney, on the other hand, lacked Max Fleischer's technical expertise, so he relied on Ubbe's inventiveness to help him realise his vision. They discovered the solution by photographing Virginia against a white backdrop. After the live-action was finished, the photographs were printed and animated characters and scenery were painted on a cell where there was white space. After photographing the cels, the two prints - the live-action film and the animated film - were combined into a single reel.

As Walt realised he would be able to complete Alice's Wonderland without running out of money, he began looking for a distributor. When he mentioned his new endeavour to Milton Feld, general manager of the Newman Theater, Feld advised him to contact Margaret Winkler, distributor of Sullivan's Felix the Cat cartoons. Walt lost little time in writing a letter on May 14, proclaiming something never seen before in the medium of animation. He went on to say that his video would appeal to everyone, regardless of class or age, and that he would have a finished print ready to transmit within a few weeks. Winkler responded, excited at the potential of a new series.

Unfortunately, production quickly slipped behind schedule. Shortly after delivering the letter to Winkler, the McConahay Building was purchased by a new landlord, Clifford Collingsworth, who quickly discovered that the Laugh-O-gram studios had a history of nonpayment of rent. To make up for the money owed, the new owner placed a lien on the studio's belongings, including the furniture and art supplies, and then locked the entrance to prevent anyone from entering until the rent was paid. Walt and his colleagues were eventually allowed back into their offices to take the studio's equipment and furniture and transport it to the nearby Wirthman Building, which housed office space as well as the Isis Theater, where the Martha Song-O-Reel had debuted.

Walt, who had become fond of his mouse buddies during his tenure at the McConahay Building, concluded that the Wirthman's proprietors would not enjoy any more rodents. He carried them in a small box to adjacent Swope Park, where he chose a remote wooded location, placed the box on the ground, and gently flipped it over, allowing the mice to escape. Mortimer and his companions crawled out of the cage at first, sniffing the ground around them. They came to a halt a little distance away from the cage and gazed up at him, as if to ask what he wanted them to do: they had been somewhat domesticated during their time with the young guy. Indeed, a number of the mice dashed back to the box, waiting for their friend to retrieve it and bring them to the studio. Walt, once again saddened by loss, had to shoo the mice away and take the box up to keep them from returning, before turning around and walking away.

More Disney artists, like Rudy Ising and Carman Maxwell, left Laugh-O-gram, discouraged by their ongoing decline. Later that summer, business manager Jack Kloepper not only departed the company, but also sued for back pay; Walt avoided the summons by being at the studio when a police officer arrived to serve the warrant. Hugh Harman, who had been at Walt's side since they worked together at the Kansas City Film Ad Company, maintained himself and his friend by using money obtained from his father on a weekly basis to keep himself and Walt up at the neighbouring Elsmere Hotel.

Walt was embarrassed even more when, on June 18, he wrote a letter to Winkler explaining that the studio was behind schedule on Alice's Wonderland, blaming it on a variety of delays, unforeseen events, and the recent move into the Wirthman Building. Walt pledged to finish the film as soon as possible, even going so far as to say he'd be in New York City, print in hand, around July 1st to sign a contract with her.

Walt, nearing the end of his rope, wrote to Roy in California, detailing everything. "Kid, you gotta get out of there," Roy replied quickly. "I don't think there's anything else you can do to save it."

Walt was devastated. This goal, which he had followed for the past few years since starting at Pesmen-Rubin, appeared to have come to an end. Walt declared bankruptcy and began liquidating his possessions, deciding to take Roy's advice and relocate to California, where he could start again. Walt went door-to-door in the nearby neighbourhoods, offering to take films of young couples' children in order to purchase a train ticket to move west. He soon had enough money to buy a train ticket and sell his camera, which he used to pay off some of his debts, including those owed to the owners of the Forest Inn Café.

Walt had dinner with Edna Francis the night before he left Kansas City in late July 1923. While he had lost everything, including his goals, Edna noted that he was ecstatic about the chances Hollywood offered, talking nonstop about how he would quit animation in favour of a position as a film director.

The next morning, he went to the home of Louise Rast, his brother Herbert's mother-in-law, to prepare for his voyage. Mrs Rast offered Walt some food for the train and even gave him a suit that no longer fit one of her kids to make him look more presentable. Soon after, a Rast family friend arrived to take Walt to Union Station.

After a brief period in the North Waiting Room, the following statement was made: "Now boarding the Santa Fe, California Limited for Los Angeles and all points in between!"" Walt entered the west side of the hall via the doors and down the wooden steps to the platform below. As he boarded the train and made his way into first class - he had decided to start the next era of his life on a confident note - he most likely got a few sidelong stares because he was dressed casually in black-and-white chequered trousers, a matching jacket, and a brown cardigan sweater. Mrs Rast's nicer attire was packed in a well-used cardboard suitcase by his side, together with the few pairs of socks and underwear he still possessed and a tin print of Alice in Wonderland. A wad of cash totaling $40 was put into his pocket, which he hoped would be enough to get him by.

Walt peered out the window of his top bed in the first-class compartment at the platform below. It had always reminded him of the loss he had felt with the departure of his parents and sister, but this time he felt no sadness.

Only excitement for what was to come.

PART VII: THE FIRST ANIMATED CARTOON STUDIO IN HOLLYWOOD – LOS ANGELES, CALIFORNIA, 1923–1928

Chapter Nineteen: Alice

Arriving in Los Angeles, Walt Disney started a new chapter, living with his Uncle Robert in Los Feliz and seeking film work. Despite initial setbacks, including rejection from studios and a rained-out film extra role, Walt remained determined. The bankruptcy of Laugh-O-gram Films weighed on him, but he shifted focus to creating gag reels for Alexander Pantages' theatres.

Walt's perseverance led to a contract with Margaret Winkler for a series based on "Alice's Wonderland." His brother Roy joined him, overcoming tuberculosis, and they formed Disney Bros. Studio. Financial challenges persisted, but they managed to hire staff and create popular Alice Comedies, despite disagreements with distributor Charles Mintz over payments and film content.

Walt's personal life flourished with his marriage to Lillian Bounds. Professionally, he innovated in animation techniques and storytelling, but struggled with financial constraints and declining interest in the Alice series. As the series ended, Mintz proposed a new rabbit character for Universal, marking a pivotal moment in Walt's career and the animation industry.

Chapter Twenty: Oswald

Over the next few weeks, Walt and Ub collaborated on creating a new rabbit character for Universal. It was decided that it would be taller than Julius the Cat, with long ears and large feet, not only to distinguish him as a rabbit, but also to distinguish him from other cartoon creatures seen in theatres. Ub also said that the rounder contours of the rabbit make him easier to animate than Julius' sharper angles. Walt was noncommittal when he submitted the sketches to Mintz, simply delivering the concepts to Universal.

After studying the drawings, Laemmle expressed his enthusiasm and submitted a contract to Mintz to function as the go-between. The arrangement, signed on March 4, 1927, called for Mintz to pay for twenty-six animated shorts utilising the rabbit character at $2,250 each feature.

The new character's name has yet to be determined. Walt and his team brainstormed several ideas and presented them to Universal, who made the final decision. When the names arrived at Laemmle's office, they were placed into a hat, and the winning name was drawn out by P.D. Universal's vice president of advertising, Cochrane. Oswald the Lucky Rabbit was the moniker given to the new character.

Meanwhile, when the Walt Disney Studios completed its final Alice comedy, Ub was hard at work on the first Oswald feature. Poor Papa was completed in two weeks by Ub and his crew of animators, which included Harman, Ising, and Freleng. Walt made several ideas and criticisms, and the animators went back to work making changes before the completed film was printed and transported to Mintz in New York on April 10. The short starred Oswald as a new father who was overwhelmed by the overwhelming quantity of young bunnies delivered by his wife. Over the following few minutes, Oswald grows increasingly enraged as he pursues his new kids and daughters around, many of them causing mischief or destruction. He climbs to his roof, shotgun in hand, and begins firing at a swarm of storks about to drop more babies down the chimney. As the animation concludes, the new father collapses against a wall, hand on his brow, resigned to his new role as provider for dozens of children.

Charles Mintz was enraged by what he witnessed. He sent a frantic note to Walt, noting that Oswald was not being portrayed as a hero that spectators could rally around, and that he was becoming lost in the film's cast of characters, which included a doctor, Oswald's wife, the children, and an army of storks. He was also embarrassed by what Disney came up with because, as he noted, Oswald's character wasn't that distinct from the other cartoon characters on the market. Instead, he proposed that Oswald be "young, snappy, and wearing a monocle." Universal concurred with Mintz, telling Walt that Oswald was obese and old-looking. Hal Hodes, the sales director of Universal's Short Product & Complete Service Departments, noted in a letter dated 15 April that the animation was jerky and repetitious, that Oswald was not a hilarious figure, and that the gags in the picture were unrelated and didn't push the tale along. As a result, Universal opted not to release Poor Papa in theatres.

Walt was devastated. In response to Mintz's letter, he stated that he accepted Hodes' concerns, referring to them as "constructive criticism." He went on to apologise to Mintz and Universal for Poor Papa's disappointment, stating that he was uncomfortable with the finished result and assured Mintz that the character and manner of storytelling will be revisited in the next instalment.

As Ub and Walt sat down and looked at the character, it was literally back to the drawing board. What distinguishes Oswald the Lucky Rabbit from other cartoons on the market? They questioned themselves. It was determined that they wished for Oswald to have his own on-screen personality, one that was cranky, highly energetic, whose emotions were clear, and who handled issues in a distinctively inventive manner. To capture this personality, they somewhat altered the character's appearance, making him appear younger and thinner than he did in Poor Papa. They also established that Oswald would not produce gags by misbehaving, but would rather respond to events unfolding around him in a creative way that would result in a gag.

Using this new approach to the character, Ub swiftly began work on the second Oswald picture, Trolley Troubles, finishing it in two weeks for shipment to Mintz on May 1. Universal was considerably satisfied with the second Oswald film, electing to debut it on July 4 at Los Angeles' Criterion Theater and on July 9 at New York's Roxy Theater before going into full distribution on September 5 across the country. Reviewers adored Oswald the Lucky Rabbit, claiming that audiences burst out laughing at the on-screen action, and Universal's internal newsletter dubbed the short film a "sensation." Across America, theatre marquees began to hawk 'Oswald the Lucky Rabbit,' which drew just as many people as feature films. Charles Mintz, who was jealous that Walt Disney was getting all the glory, explained to him that the true credit should go to George Winkler, who had started hanging out around the studio, delivering messages from his brother-in-law and even occasionally consulting on the films.

Walt had finally found the success he had sought since his introduction into the film industry in 1921. With the popularity of Trolley Troubles, the Walt Disney Studio began producing new animated films every two weeks, paying Mintz the agreed-upon fee of $2,250 per picture. To keep up with their schedule, Walt began employing more animators and ink-and-paint artists, growing his workforce from ten to twenty-two by the end of 1927. During this period, Walt drew heavily on his Kansas City fan base, rehiring Ham Hamilton and Carman Maxwell, as well as Les Clark, a new artist searching for a break in the industry. With the added pressure of creating a popular and successful series, Walt's expectations for his crew rose, much to the dismay of his artists. As a result, he had little sympathy for Rudy Ising, firing the young man with whom he'd worked for years when Rudy fell asleep while photographing one of the films.

Recognizing the short timetable that releasing a film every two weeks demanded, Walt made significant changes to his studio's organisation. Production was split into two different units, with his best animators, Ub Iwerks and Hugh Harman, in charge of each. He also established a more formalised procedure for creating animated shorts. After typing out the script for each one, Ub and Harman created rough sketches of the action in each scene so that the animators assigned to a sequence could see how it would go.

More characters were created to accompany Oswald on his exploits as the story progressed. Some characters from the Alice Comedies were reused, such as the dachshund, police dog, and recurring villain, renamed Putrid Pete instead of Bootleg Pete. Recognizing the need for a love interest for Oswald, a female rabbit named Fanny was created, which introduced a whole new dimension of humour as the film's protagonist was continuously fighting for her attention, resulting in a slew of laughs. After the sixth Oswald film, All Wet, an unknown female cat took her position as his love interest till the end of the series.

The plots of the Oswald films differed. While Oswald's characteristics and personality remained intact across the films, the cartoon rabbit's roles changed from feature to picture. In July's Oh Teacher, for example, Oswald portrayed a kid defending his sweetheart from a playground bully. In December's Harem Scarem, Oswald was a traveller who fell in love with a belly dancer while visiting a Moroccan café. While the films were frequently situational comedies, the humour and details were frequently drawn from news and current events. In September's Rickety Gin, for example, Oswald portrays a cop who goes up against Putrid Pete, the leader of a bootleg whiskey gang in prohibition-era America.

As Oswald's fame grew, Universal began to actively promote him with an intensive marketing campaign. Consumers began to see Lucky Rabbit-themed merchandise, such as a milk chocolate candy bar made by Portland's Vogan Candy Company. The bar became extremely famous and was advertised in the windows of drug shops and in newspapers, only adding to Walt Disney's character's appeal.

As the studio's personnel grew and the press continued to laud his praises, Walt Disney Studios' executive began to believe that his work was worth more than what Mintz was paying him. Aside from the continual criticism of his works, the distributor became irritated when Walt began playing hardball, proposing that the price of each film be raised to $2,500.

Unbeknownst to Walt, Mintz directed George Winkler to begin arranging covert meetings with Walt's animators in the nights, sowing seeds of doubt in their minds that their employer was creating a hostile work environment. Winkler stated that Oswald's recent success was making Walt paranoid and abusive, prepared to go to any length to ensure his own success at the expense of his colleagues, citing the recent firing of Rudy Ising.

As the Walt Disney Studios top artist, Ub was one of the first asked by Winkler to turn against his boss. However, Ub's commitment to his comrade, which dated back to their time at Pesmen-Rubin, triumphed over the distributor's lies. He described the secret encounters to Walt, who, in his arrogance, refused to trust what his friend told him and pretended to be unconcerned.

Walt and Lillian's married life was still going well. When he presented her with a wrapped hatbox on Christmas Day 1927, their house felt even more like a home. The gift shifted and moved in Lillian's hands when Walt handed it to her, feeling considerably heavier than she anticipated a hat to be. As she proceeded to untie the ribbon that held the lid on, she made a slight scratching and sobbing sounds from within the box. She exclaimed as she raised the lid to reveal a little puppy inside the box. Sunnee, the new addition to the household, was named by Lillian when she fell in love with the tiny Chow.

Meanwhile, as the first series of twenty-six Oswald films came to an end, Walt decided it was time to start negotiating the next series with Mintz: if Universal expected the Walt Disney Studios to continue producing Oswald the Lucky Rabbit at the same high quality, the price delivered per film would have to rise. Walt decided that seeing Mintz in person rather than sending telegrams would be the best way to handle what he expected to be contentious discussions. As a result, Walt and Lillian Disney boarded a train to New York City in February 1928, leaving Roy in command of the studio.

Winkler had made the choice to proceed with the production of Oswald shorts without Walt's awareness. Charles Mintz signed a new three-year contract with Universal to produce Oswald shorts as Walt was travelling east by rail. Tired with Walt's incessant pleading for money and control over artistic licence, Mintz appointed George Winkler as the new head of animation for the Oswald films and directed Winkler to draft new contracts with all of the Disney artists while Walt was away. Only Ub Iwerks and Les Clark refused to betray their friend, opting to resign rather than work for Mintz.

Walt could sense something was wrong as he entered Charles Mintz's office in New York, oblivious of what was going on in Los Angeles. Sitting at the bargaining table, Walt requested that his company be paid $250 more each picture than the previous season. Mintz replied with a $1,800 offer per picture.

Walt was perplexed. He indicated that it was difficult enough for him to produce a film for $2,250 with the personnel he currently had. How could he make a high-quality film for $450 less?

Mintz stated that the offer of $1,800 per picture was still valid. Not only that, but Walt would no longer be in command of the studio, but would instead be a subcontractor reporting to George Winkler, the new head of production.

Walt went out of Charles Mintz's studio that afternoon, dazed. What had occurred? What would his reaction be? He realised he needed to contact Roy in California in order to secure his artists before Mintz's plan went into effect.

"There's a break with Charlie looming," Walt revealed to his brother in a telegraph. "Write a new contract with the boys before we're destabilised." Offer them a 10% pay rise with the option of bonuses. "Don't worry, everything is fine," Walt said, but it was too late.

When Walt returned to Mintz's office the next day, he threatened to find a new distributor for the Oswald films unless he received the $2,500 per film he demanded. Mintz burst up laughing in his face. Walt indicated that he couldn't legally negotiate with another studio without ol' Charlie Mintz. Mintz owned Oswald the Lucky Rabbit, not Walt Disney Studios.

Walt Disney could only do so much. While he co-created Oswald the Lucky Rabbit with Ub Iwerks and his name was on the studio that produced the shorts, cinema distributors owned the character in the early twentieth century. This meant that, legally, ever since Poor Papa debuted in 1927, Oswald and his twenty-six animated shorts belonged to Mintz rather than Walt.

Walt saw that Mintz had triumphed because of his naiveté. Standing in the distributor's office doorway, he admitted defeat and told Mintz he could have Oswald. The young artist had one more thing to give his scheming previous distributor: sage advice.

"Watch your back, Charlie," he said. "If the boys abandoned me, they'll abandon you," Walt predicted to Mintz. In 1929, Universal parted relations with Charles Mintz, giving the series to Walter Lantz, whom Mintz had engaged to direct the Oswald cartoons after stealing the character from Walt Disney. Until 1938, Lantz and Universal continued to produce new Oswald the Lucky Rabbit cartoons.

Walt didn't need to tell his wife anything when he returned to the hotel to see Lillian: she could tell by his demeanour that the fight was over.

"Let's get out of this hellhole," he said. He returned to Roy after stopping by the Western Union office at a New York train station: LEAVING TONIGHT, STOPPING OVER IN KANSAS CITY. EVERYTHING OK.

Walt and Lillian boarded the New York Central Cannonball back to Los Angeles. Walt was a different man after his final conversation with Charles Mintz. He'd arrived in New York City feeling like the richest man in the world due to his success with Oswald only two weeks ago, but he was coming home bankrupt, realising he'd possessed nothing. He realised that the only person one could fully trust in this world was oneself. He resolved that he would never work for another individual again in his life.

Walt Disney felt like he was leaving his aspirations behind as the New York Central Cannonball followed the sun westward towards Los Angeles on March 13, 1928.

The 26-year-old artist had five days to stew over the injustice done to him by the artists he'd most trusted and Charles Mintz. While he had been betrayed, he had concluded that finishing the current season of Oswald cartoons would be the appropriate thing to do. If all went as planned, the final animated picture, Hot Dog, would be completed and presented to Universal on August 3.

The conductor stepped into the first-class cabin a few evenings after Walt and Lillian left New York and announced that they would be stopping in a little town called Marceline to refuel; passengers were welcome to step off the train to stretch on the platform, even though it was the middle of the night.

Walt debated whether or not to get off the train. Marceline was very special to him. It taught him the value of hard work, discipline, and community. He scoffed to himself, "Those lessons did me some good." Despite the fact that he had been disciplined and worked hard to pursue his aspirations, they had never been his to take. Not only that, but the community he'd formed at Laugh-O-gram and the Walt Disney Studios had deserted him.

He realised that growing up in Marceline had also taught him to never give up, especially by watching his father do everything he could to keep the family farm running and persuade his neighbours to fight the banks and railroad firms. Finally, his passion for his Marceline years won him over, and he decided to give the animation business another try. He gently nudged Lillian awake and informed her he wanted to get off the train in his Marceline during their one-hour stopover to show off his small town.

The train proceeded on to Kansas City after a brief stop at Marceline, where the young couple disembarked to spend the day touring to help break up the monotony of the ride. Walt took Lillian on a tour of the city, showing her the Bellefontaine mansion, which functioned as the hub for Elias' paper route. He recalled waking up hours before daylight, sometimes in bitter cold, to deliver newspapers, and how it taught him to work hard simply because it was the proper thing to do, even in the face of adversity. They drove by the Scottish Rite temple, where Walt was admitted as a DeMolay in 1920, and where Dad Land ingrained in him the value of fidelity, civility, comradeship, and creativity. Walt even took the time to show his wife where he worked for Pesmen-Rubin, Kansas City Film Ad Company, and finally the Laugh-O-gram studio, explaining how he began as a simple lettering artist and worked his way up to become one of Kansas City's premier producers of animated shorts.

As their time in Kansas City came to a conclusion, the couple made their way through the Grand Hall and into Union Station's North Waiting Room. Walt recalls visiting Union Station every week for years to bathe because he didn't have running water otherwise due to his homelessness.

Standing beneath the enormous luminous clock, Walt realised he needed to make a major decision quickly. His decision had two outcomes, but only one could be chosen: should he simply abandon his dream, potentially leading Lillian and himself into financial ruin, as he had done while living in the Laugh-O-gram studio, or would he choose to work hard, overcome adversity, and use his creativity to press forward and change the path to achieving his dream?

Walt had made his decision as the pair walked through the west doors of the North Waiting Room, down the wooden stairway to the platforms below, and aboard the train that would take them home to Los Angeles.

But how will he get there? How would he restart and rise from the ashes to become somebody in the world of animation once more?

As the train began to move west out of Kansas City, it went through a small forest of trees. He recalls having fun with his artists at Swope Park when operating Laugh-O-gram and releasing his pet mice into the park when he chose to relocate to California.

Mice. Nobody had ever made a moving mouse before.

"I'm thinking about making a new character," Walt said to Lillian. "It's a mouse." I'll refer to him as Mortimer."

"Mortimer? "That doesn't sound right," Lillian commented.

Walt cocked his brow. His wife sat peacefully, gazing out the window at the trees flying by. She offered another suggestion as she turned to face Walt.

"How about Mickey?""

Made in United States
Troutdale, OR
10/21/2024